The 'Parents' Time Off' Series

KIDS' FUN CRAFT ACTIVITIES

Cecilia Egan

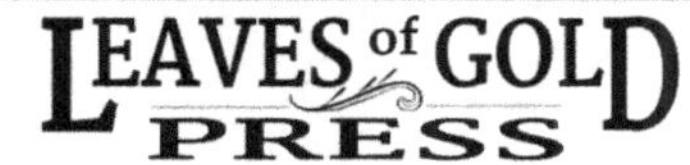

First published in 1989 by Ashton Egan
as Australian Kids'Crafts

Revised and updated 2015

National Library of Australia Cataloguing-in-Publication entry

Creator: Egan, Cecilia, author, illustrator.

Title: Kids' fun craft activities / Cecilia Egan.

Edition: 2nd edition

ISBN: 9781925110722 (paperback)

Series: Parents' time off series ; 5.

Target Audience: For primary school age (6-12 year old)

Subjects: Creative activities and seat work.

Handicraft for children.

Handicraft--Juvenile literature.

Dewey Number: 745.5083

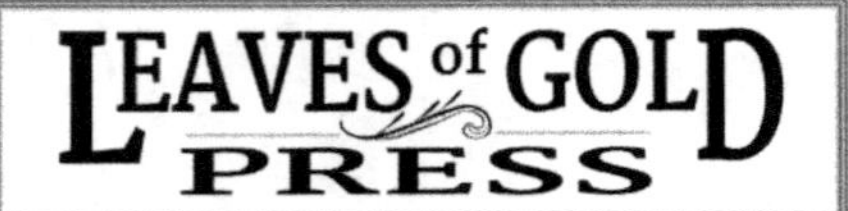

ABN 67 099 575 078

PO Box 345, Shoreham, 3916, Victoria, Australia
www.leavesofgoldpress.com

CONTENTS

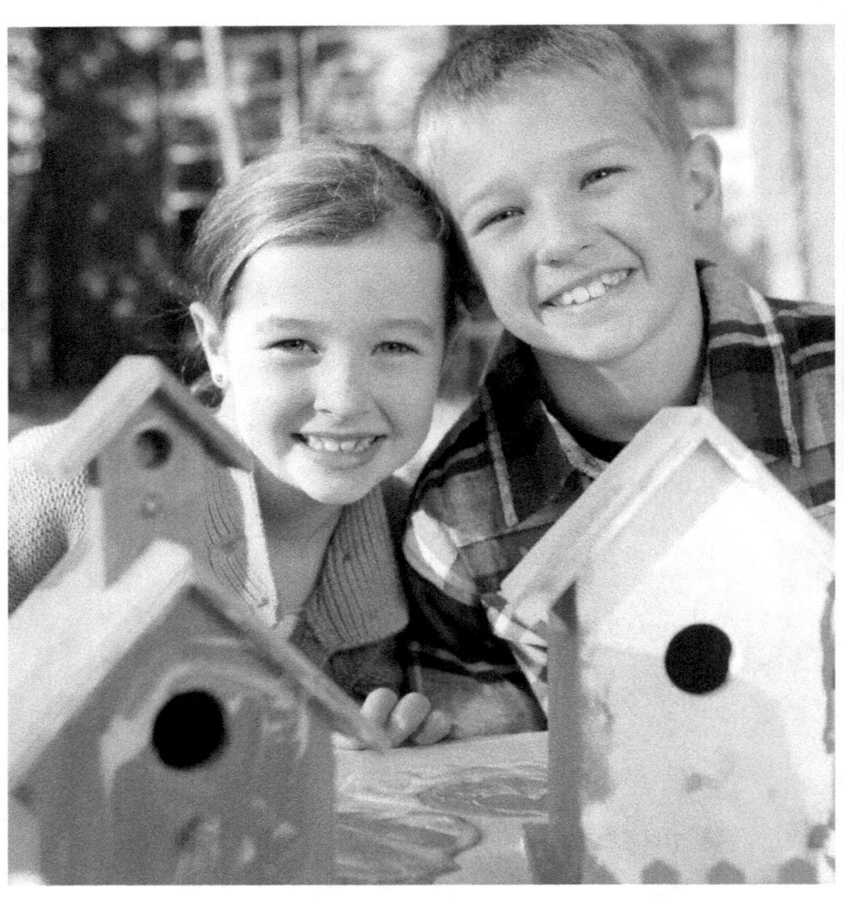

Introduction

To the Kids:

Crafts are exciting! This book shows you how to make lots of different things to use, to decorate your house, to give as gifts or to show your friends. Choose something you like and have fun making it. Invite friends and family members to make something with you!

To the Parents:

Crafts are much more than just a way to pass the time – they are valuable educational tools. Activities that are suited to a child's age and level of development can encourage learning in a wide variety of areas, such as art, language, music, science and maths.

Craft activities are a good way for children (and adults) to express their creativity and develop fine motor skills. They can help us understand such concepts as color theory, the alphabet, measurement and numbers, and experience scientific process in a multitude of ways. For example, baking home-made modelling clay to make picture frames involves the changing properties of flour when it is mixed with water, and sticking objects together involves the alteration of glue's characteristics as it dries.

These activities encourage children to use their imagination to invent their own entertainment. Making something all by themselves gives them self-esteem, and helps them gain confidence in their own abilities.

Children love doing craft activities. To ensure they continue to enjoy and benefit from them parents must be aware of some cautions.

Choose a craft project that is suited to the child's level of development.

If a project turns out to be too hard, children can be discouraged. Make sure your child has the skills needed for a particular project.

Start with the basics.

If your child is trying a craft for the first time, make sure he or she begins with a very simple project. This will help the child become familiar with techniques, and with using the tools and materials.

Provide the right space and plenty of time.

Craft activities take up space – give children access to a large table or bench, and even some shelves on which to keep the materials.

Crafts can sometimes appear to be messy. Don't fret – this is all part of the experience. Provide a 'wet area' for extra messy projects, or even arrange a space for them outdoors. If you are constantly worried about paint spilling on your carpet, the project will not be fun for anyone.

And if the project takes several days, be prepared to have materials on display during that time. Insisting that everything be packed away every evening even when the project is unfinished, can be time-consuming and disconcerting.

Some projects don't take long but others require more time. There is no need to hurry things along. Give your child time to think the project through, to become immersed in it, to experiment, to invent and to really have fun. Pushing them to 'hurry up' will detract from their creativity and enjoyment.

Never force kids to finish a project they have lost interest in.
Craft should be fun – not a duty or an obligation. Forcing children to do craft will extinguish their interest in craft. The parent's role is to encourage them and allow them to do things for themselves. This will help boost their confidence.

With craft activities, parents and guardians can help children learn while having fun - and that is the best way!

HOME-MADE MODELLING CLAY

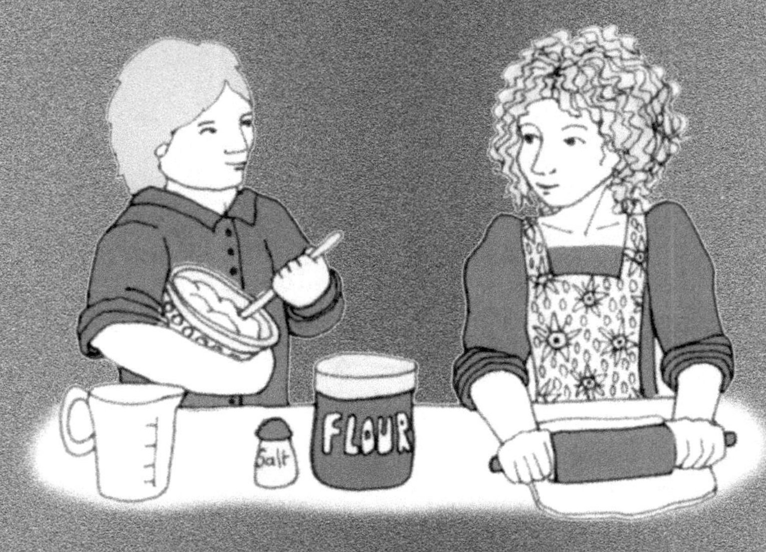

HOME-MADE MODELLING CLAY

Materials:

2 cups plain (all-purpose) flour
¾ cup cooking salt
About ½ cup water

Instructions:

Mix the sifted flour with all the salt. Then with a knife or spoon make a well in the centre. Slowly add the water into the well as you mix this into a firm dough. If the mixture is too sticky, add flour. If it is too dry, add more water. Knead the clay until it is a good consistency for modelling.

After you make your model, bake it for four hours in a low oven 100°C (200°F) gas or electric.

Allow your model to cool completely before you paint it. When the paint is dry, home-made modelling clay models must be thickly varnished on all sides to prevent them from going soggy.

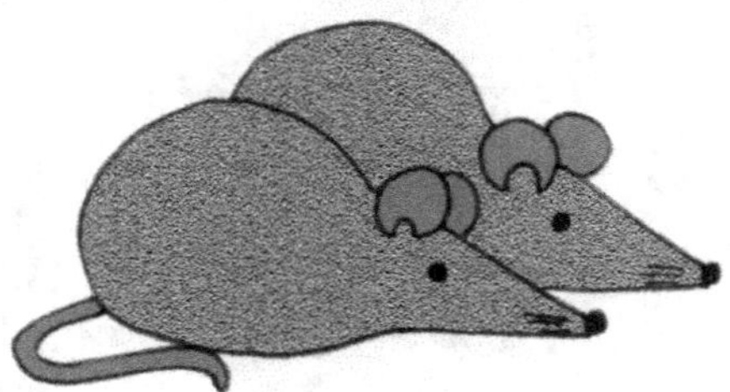

MODELLING CLAY MICE

Materials:

Home-made modelling clay
Varnish
Toothpicks
Large gumnuts/seedpods
Acrylic paint

Step 1: Butter an oven tray to put your mice on. Roll a small amount of clay into a ball, making a point at the end for the face. Then roll a tiny ball and stick it at the end of the point for the actual nose. You can put something equally small in for the nose such as a tiny pebble or gumnut as long as it is not meltable. Attach a larger ball of clay for the body.

Step 2: Roll out two small balls, and flatten them out for the ears. Put them on the head. Then roll two tiny balls and stick them on for the eyes. With a toothpick, poke a hole in the middle for pupils. Roll a thin worm for the tail, attach it to the back. With a toothpick engrave three small lines on each side of the nose for whiskers.

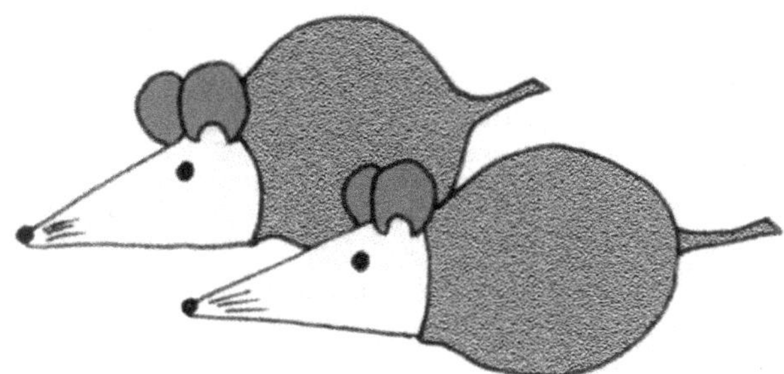

Step 3: The mice also look attractive made with large gumnuts (eucalyptus tree seedpods). Do this before you start the details on the mouse. Push the clay firmly around the gumnuts so that the gumnut forms the body and the clay forms the head. Leave the stems on the gumnuts for tails. Bake in a low oven for four hours.

Step 4: Leave the mice to cool and then you can paint the pupils in black the ears grey and pink and the nose black. You can even paint spots or lines on the body for an interesting effect. Once you have painted them, brush on varnish, at least two to three coats, to avoid cracking.

MODELLING CLAY BROOCHES

Materials:

Home-made modelling clay
Strong glue
Brooch pins
Acrylic Paint
Varnish

TINY PEOPLE BROOCHES

Step 1: Making brooches has to be done carefully as being so small, they are a bit tricky. Make a rather small ball about 1 sq. cm. Attach another ball about half the size of this on top, for the head.

Step 2: With a toothpick poke eyes, a nose, a smile and two eyebrows. Flatten a small round ball and stick this on top of the head as a hat. Onto the side of the hat stick two tiny balls on one side and one on the other. Make a hole in the middle of these balls with the round end of the toothpick. These represent tiny seedpods. If you like you can use real ones.

Step 3: Make about four holes down the middle of the big ball to represent buttons. Then roll two small arms and two small legs. Make a line to show where the hands and feet are. Attach these onto the body.

Step 4: Cook and once cooled, paint in colours such as red, pink, brown etc. The face should be left unpainted, for a better effect. Paint the hands and feet a different colour from the arms and legs.

(Actual size)

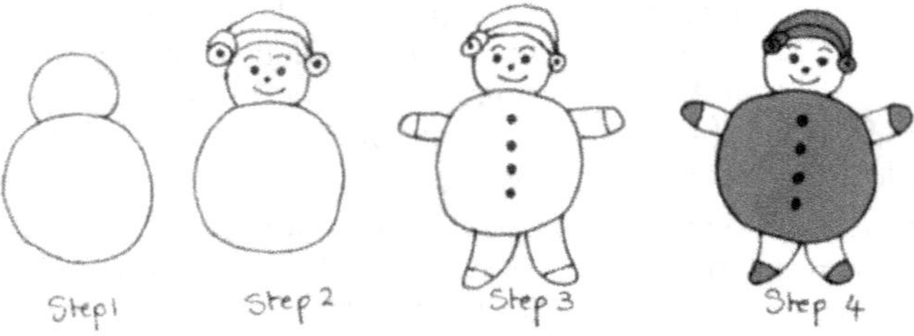

BROOCH SHAPES

You can cut out the shape you want with paper then trace around it cutting the modelling clay. You can make love-hearts — striped or spotted. Stars also look good.

Letters are great, but you must keep in mind that you have to fit the brooch pin on — so letters such as "T" and "L" are fine but "S" and "O" are a bit harder to make.

For a nice finish, varnish the brooches.

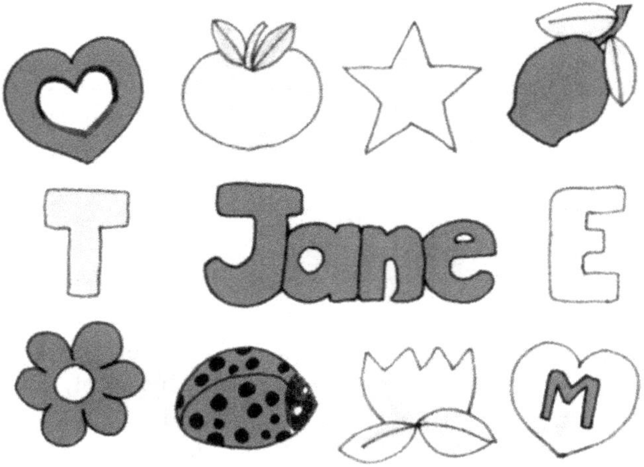

BREAD BASKET

Materials:

Home-made modelling clay
Poppy and sesame seeds
Medium sized basket
Two or three dried flowers
Two or three stalks of dried wheat or fox tails plant
Ribbon
Sacking/hessian/burlap material or other fabric

Step 1: Making miniature bread is just as easy as making normal bread. First there is the French stick which is a long roll. Dab on some water and dip it into a plate of sesame seeds. Once you have done this, with an icy-pole stick or something similar, press in light lines going across the French stick diagonally.

Step 2: Then make a larger football shape. Make lines on this like you did with the French stick, and dip it in poppy seeds. This makes a loaf of bread.

Step 3: Make some small plaited rolls and some round buns, and some small long rolls. Tiny knot rolls are easy to make by simply rolling out a thin roll about 4 cm (1 ½ inches) long and tying it in a knot. You can put sesame or poppy seeds on any bread you like. Keep your eyes open and you'll discover all the sorts of bread shapes you can make.

Step 4: Once you have made your miniature breads, line them up on a greased tray and cook them for four hours in a low oven, 125°C (250°F). Leave them to cool, and be sure to varnish them well so the sesame and poppy seeds don't rot.

Step 5: Cut out the material (which can be flowered, checked or anything), in a rectangle, and press it into the basket then arrange the bread attractively and glue it in. Put the dried wheat in with the bread, sticking out of the basket. Tie a short ribbon on the handle and curl it. Glue two or three tiny, coloured dried flowers onto the ribbon.

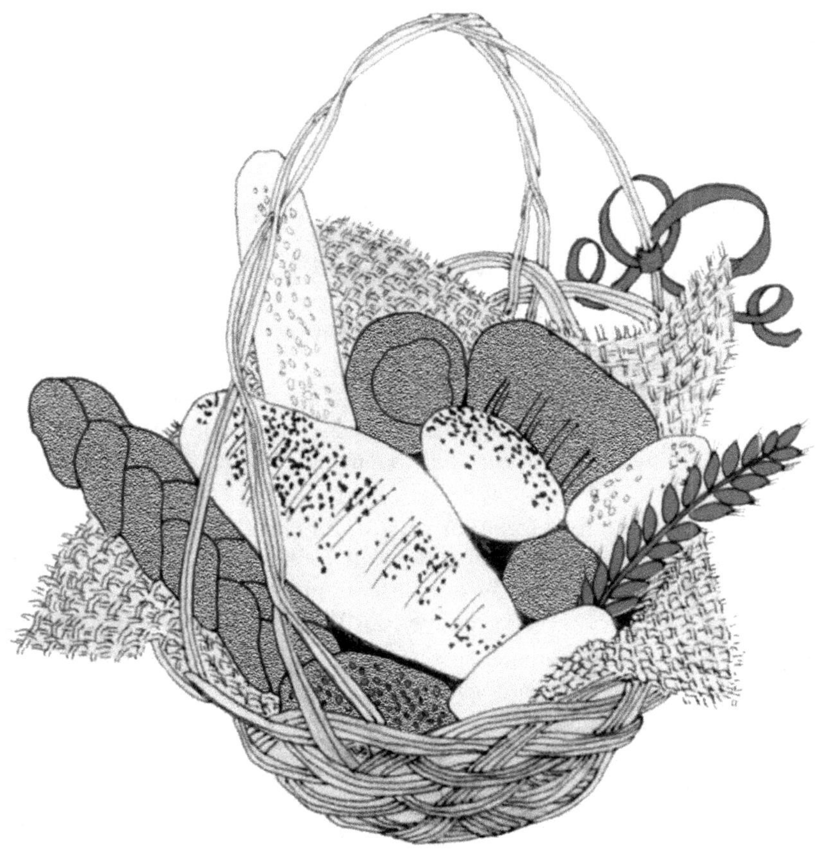

DOLL WALL PLAQUES

Materials:

Home-made modelling clay
Garlic crusher
A toothpick
Acrylic paint
Varnish

Step 1: For the head roll a ball about 3½ cm (1½ inches) or a bit smaller. Then with your fingers softly press two round dents in the middle of the head. Make two tiny balls and put them in the center of the two dents. With a toothpick press two holes in the middle for pupils. Roll a circle for the nose, and engrave a smile and eyebrows. The hair comes later.

Step 2: Mould a thick roll for her chest and attach the head onto it. Then cut out two shapes for her shirt and attach this to the chest. Cut out a rectangle and stick this on the skirt as an apron. Put a thin roll around the waist.

Step 3: Attach two rolls to either side of the chest for arms. Make a thin strip and put it around the top of the arms for short sleeves. Make a bow and collar on the top of the chest. Flatten out the tips of the arms to make hands, and with a toothpick engrave four lines to represent fingers.

Step 4. Now comes the hair. Push some modelling clay through a garlic crusher and stick the strands to the sides of the head with a few short ones for the fringe. Put a bow or a hat in the hair. Add a bangle or two to the arms. Make a basket of fruit in her hands, or make a pocket on her apron, with one hand in it.

Step 5: The feet are just two short rolls stuck under the skirt. Make boots by turning the ends of the roll into a point and putting some circles for buttons down the side. Don't forget to make a hook on the top with modelling clay, or just stick some strong wire in it for a hanger. Cook them, and paint them. Pale pinks and blues look good on dolls. You can sign your name on the bottom with a felt-tip pen and then varnish on both sides.

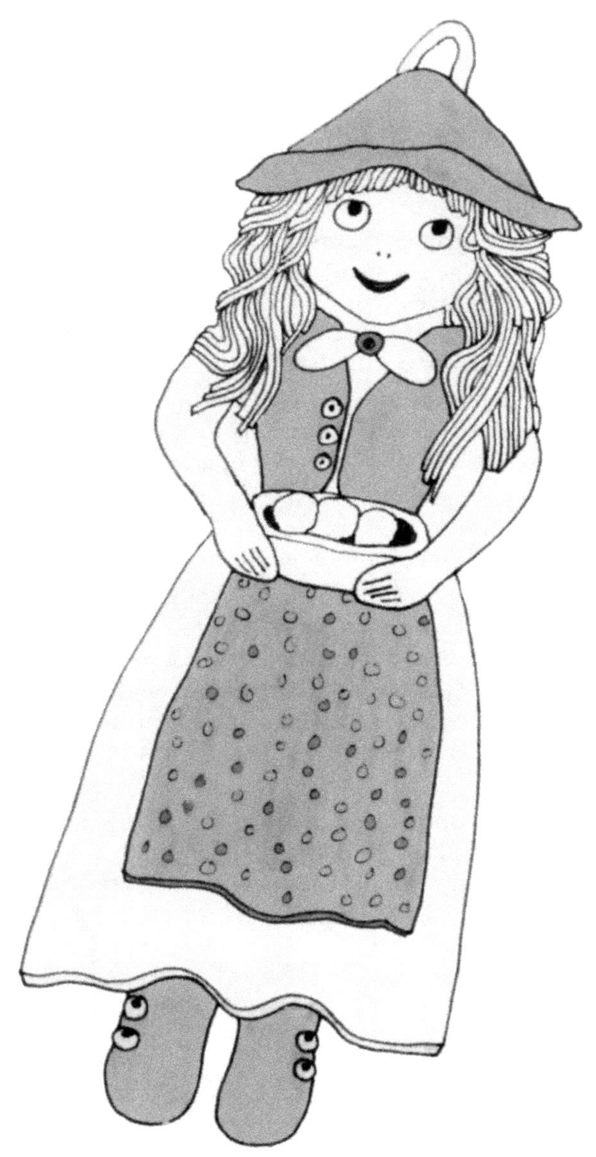

EASTER BASKETS

Materials:

Small wide basket
Ribbon
About 10 small Easter eggs
Cellophane
Large, round seedpods
Modelling clay
Acrylic paint
Varnish

Step 1: To make an Easter bunny, form a round ball. Point it slightly towards the nose. Attach a small ball on the pointy end for the nose and two balls for the eyes. With a toothpick, make two pupils. Make an open slit for the mouth. Shape out pointy ears and stick them on, with one ear curled over.

Step 2: Attach the head onto a large seedpod. Next, make a circular base out of dough. Attach two short rolls to it (the legs) and press the tips down for the paws. With a toothpick engrave four lines on the paws.

Step 3: Stick the seedpod into the base and attach two rolls for arms and make the paws with four lines for fingers. You can put the arms in any position — either just limp or, holding a card or an Easter egg.

Step 4: Your bunny is now finished and ready to be baked. Painting is an important part of the bunny. Choose a wide variety of colours such as pink, pale blue, lilac, red and grey. Paint the foot paws pale blue, and the arm paws pale pink. Paint the nose red or grey and paint on some eyebrows. The inside of the ears should be painted pink and the outside, grey.

For added effect put a few spots on the back of its head or on the tummy.

Step 5: Place your bunny in the middle of the basket on some shredded cellophane. Place the Easter eggs around it. If you like, add a card saying 'Happy Easter' with the person's name on it. Then get a large square piece of clear cellophane and place the basket in the middle. Gather the cellophane up at the top and tie with a ribbon. This makes a terrific Easter present.

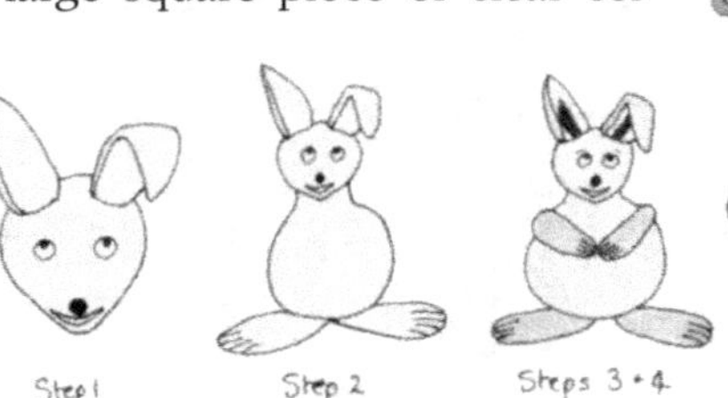

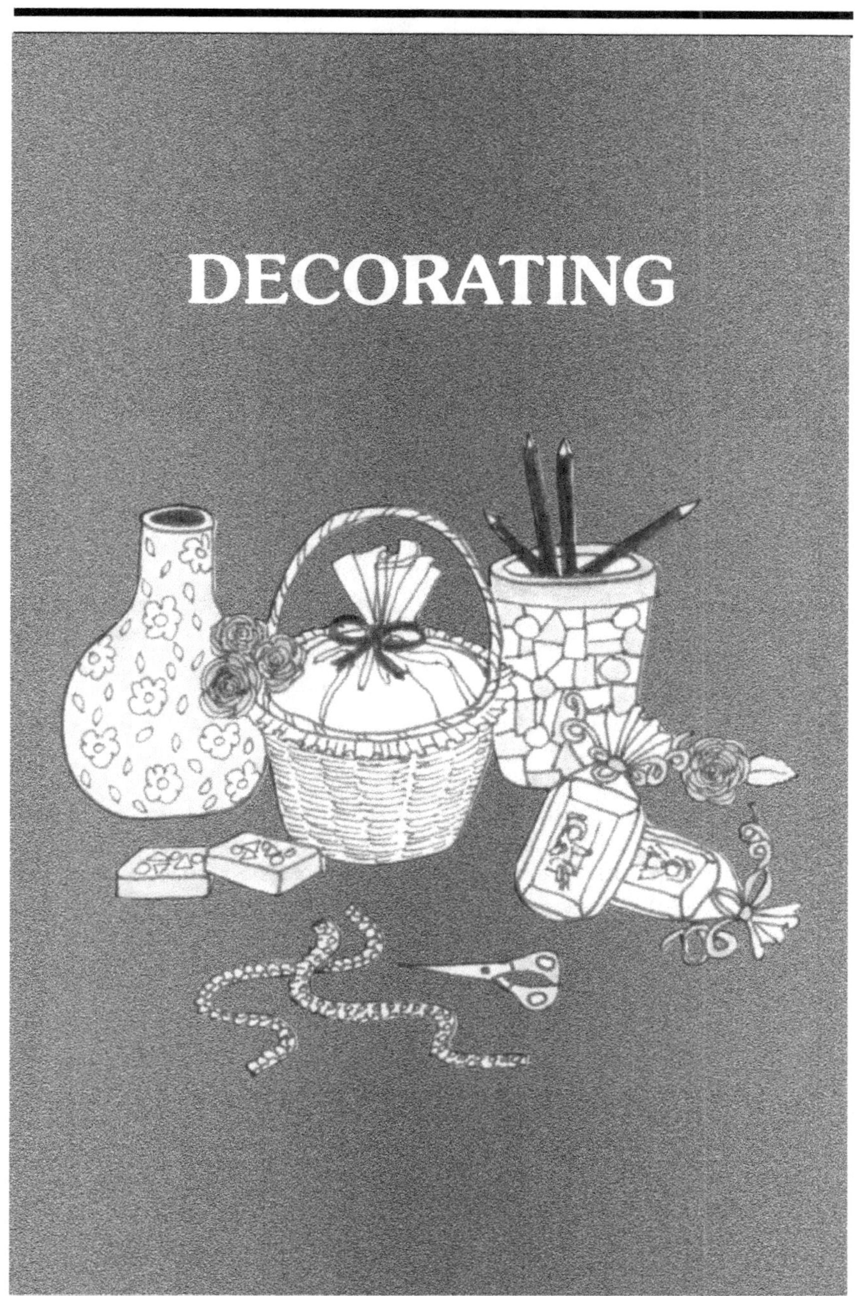
DECORATING

DECORATED BASKETS

Materials:
Plain baskets with handles
Lace and frilly trimmings
Small fake roses

To fill your baskets:
Dried lavender or potpourri
Small piece of ribbon
Fabric netting
Small soaps

Step 1: Take a piece of frilly lace and line the top of the basket with strong glue. Press the lace around the top rim of the basket over the glue. Trim off extra lace.

If this looks a bit bare, add another ring of lace a bit lower, and another.

Step 2: Once the lace has dried, take the fake roses and twist the wire stems around the handle. You can also decorate the handle by wrapping lace around it.

Step 3: Dry some lavender or make some potpourri by simply drying out some roses. (See potpourri instructions in this book.) Put some lavender or potpourri in a square of netting, gather the netting into a bag shape and tie it with a ribbon at the top. Fit it into the basket.

Step 4: If you want to put soaps in your basket, collect small coloured soaps and put them in the middle of a square piece of netting. Tie the netting up with a piece of ribbon and fit it into the basket.

Step 5: You can put both lavender and soaps into the basket. Even some hankies and perfume look good.

These baskets make great Mother's Day presents and you can put a small card in them.

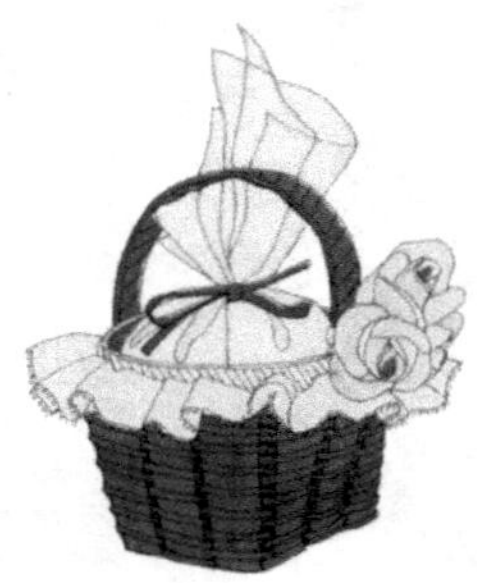

DECORATED PENCIL HOLDER JARS

Materials:

One glass jar
Coloured paper
Paper glue
Varnish
1 black felt-tip pen

Step 1: Soak the jar in a bowl of very hot water for about ten minutes. This makes it much easier to peel the label off. Wash the jar and dry it.

Step 2: With coloured paper cut out squares, triangles, stripes and circles; many shapes in many colours.

Step 3: Paint glue well, all over the shapes, and stick them onto the jar starting from the bottom, working your way upwards. Arrange large triangles with smaller ones in the middle. Try and contrast the colours.

Step 4: Once you have worked your way all around the jar paste a stripe on the rim, where the lid would screw on. After the glue has dried, trace around every shape with a black felt-tip pen. Varnish thickly, with two or three coats.

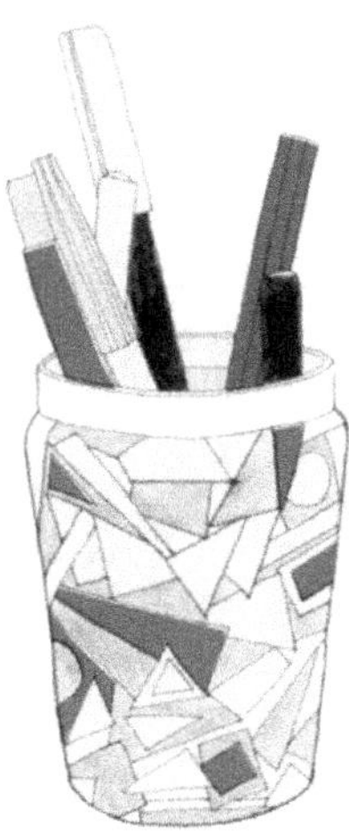

DECORATED SOAP

Materials:

Cake of soap
Scissors
Clear nail-polish or varnish
Clear cellophane
Thin ribbon
Wrapping paper

Step 1: Find or buy some wrapping paper, with small illustrations on it that would look good on soap. Make sure these illustrations aren't too complicated as you will be cutting them out. You might take the soap with you to the shop to make sure your picture is **not** too big. You may even find some small pictures in magazines e.g. flowers, boys, girls, animals, fruit etc. Once you have your picture, with small pointy scissors cut just around the outside line of the picture very carefully.

Step 2: Once you have your picture, take your soap, and with your finger dab on some water where you will want to place the picture. Put the picture on the soap and smooth out all the wrinkles — let this dry.

Step 3: Once the soap is thoroughly dry, varnish it. Paint on two coats of varnish and let this dry. While you are waiting for the varnish to dry, cut out some cellophane in a small rectangle about 18 cm by 11 cm. This can vary according to the size of the soap.

Step 4: Next comes the wrapping. There are two types of wrapping. One is done by putting the soap face down in the middle of the cellophane. Fold the long sides into the middle and with the wide sides, do the same but fold them into triangles first. This may be stuck down with glue or sticky tape. This method is just like wrapping a present. The other way is to put the soap face down near the bottom of the cellophane. Do the same as in the first method but leave the top long and open, so it is like a long bag. Then with paper ribbon tie the knot at the top and curl the ribbon with scissors.

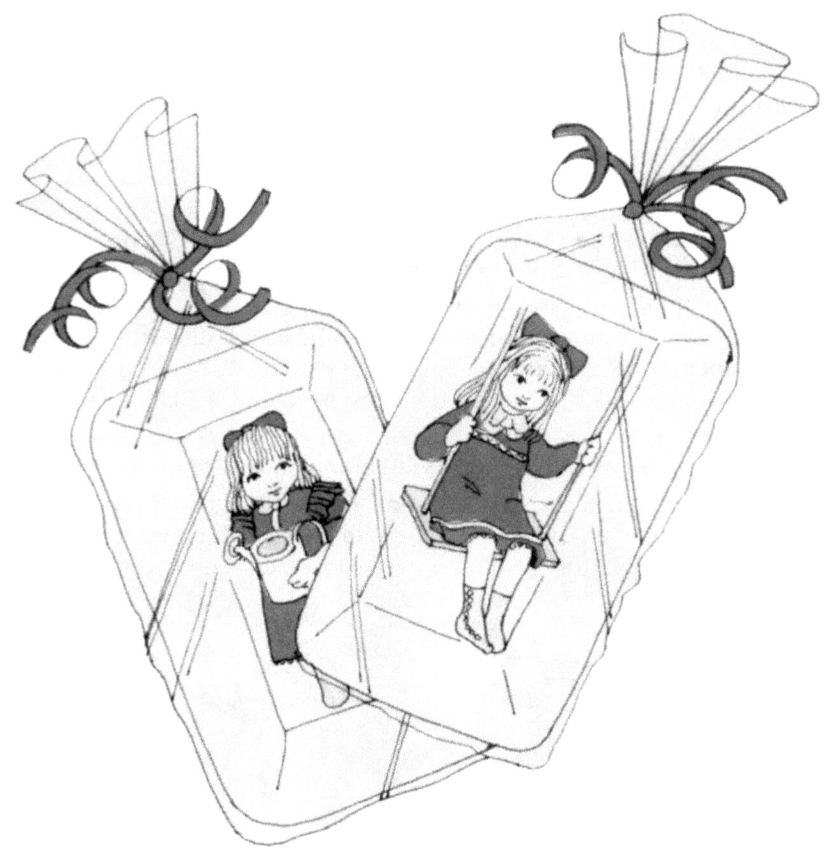

DECORATED MATCHBOXES

Materials:

Coloured paper
Wrapping paper
Clag or other paper glue
Varnish
One matchbox
Scissors

Step 1: Measure the matchbox and cut a strip the right size to cover the whole box out of coloured paper. Put clag on the paper and wrap tightly around the outside of the matchbox.

Step 2: Take out the inside of the matchbox and stick a strip of coloured paper along the rim. Cut small shapes out of coloured paper and wrapping paper. Stick these on the outside of the matchbox in a nice arrangement.

Step 3: Once it has dried, varnish the box with two or three coats.

Step 4: If your matchbox is for a pair of ear-rings or a brooch stick a small amount of cotton wool at the bottom inside of the matchbox. These boxes are great for putting small presents in, or as a jewellery box.

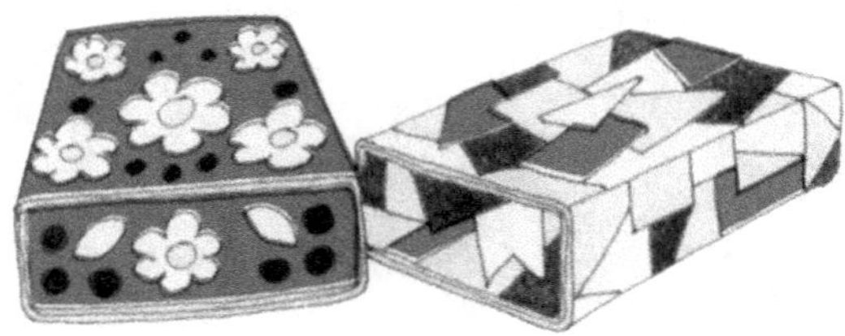

PAINTED JARS

Materials:

Oil paints
Linseed oil
Turpentine
Paint brush
Attractive jars

Step 1: Collect a lot of jars—curvy jars, vase-shaped jars, straight jars etc. Fancy jars look best. Soak them in boiling water and peel the label off. Then mix up some oil paints. Get a wooden or plastic board and on that squeeze small blobs of oil paint. The four basic colours you need are red, yellow, white and blue. Out of these you can mix any other colours you might need.

Step 2: The next step is to plan out your jar. If it is a roundish jar you might like to paint on flowers to make a vase. If so, mix up many colours for the flowers, pink, purple, orange etc. The turpentine is used for thinning the paint, to make it easier to paint with. The linseed oil makes the paint shiny.

Add a few drops of linseed oil and a few drops of turpentine. Now paint on dots in several different colours around the jar. Leave room for the petals. When painting the flowers, do not use green because the green is for the leaves.

Step 3: Now paint petals in different colours around the dots. Once you have done this fill in the extra room with more flowers or even stars and crosses. Paint on small green strokes between the flowers, to represent leaves.

Step 4: If you have a longish jar you can paint on small squares in rows all around the jar in various colours. Paint two or three rows and make sure they contrast. Then paint one or two rows of love hearts of flowers or circles, and then more squares.

Step 5: Another nice pattern is a row of butterflies around the jar. Do the middle and the wings first and wait two or three days until this dries. Then you can paint details and decoration over the wings without smudging.

Flowers look really good in these jars, and the jars are also great as pencil holders.

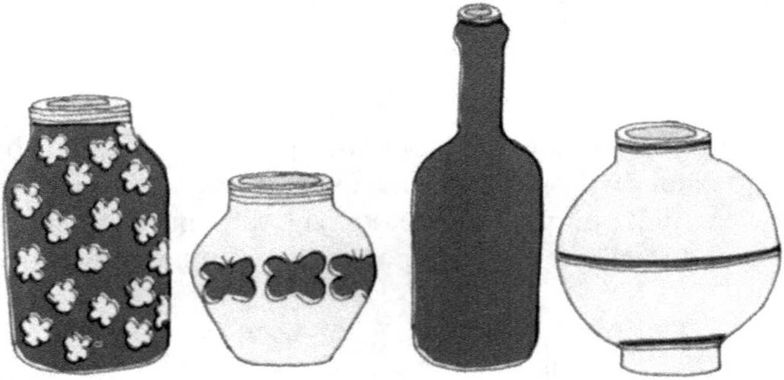

PRESSED FLOWERS

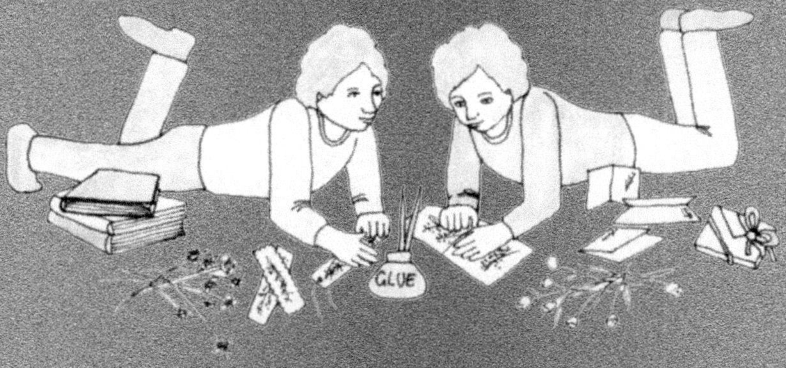

HOW TO PRESS FLOWERS AND LEAVES

Collect small flowers and thin decorative leaves such as fern leaves, from your garden. Pick them on a day when it hasn't rained — the less moisture there is, the quicker they will dry.

Fold the plants between two sheets of absorbent paper then put the papers flat under a heavy weight. A pile of books is good for pressing flowers. The plants will take a week or more to dry.

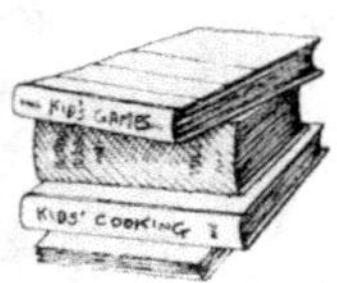

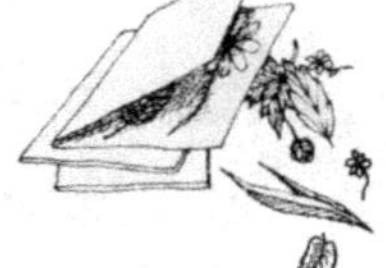

PRESSED FLOWER BOOKMARKS

Materials:

Coloured cardboard (not too thin)
Clear self-adhesive laminating plastic, e.g. CONTACT ®
A piece of cord or ribbon
Pressed flowers, dried grasses, seeds or tiny pods
Scissors or pinking shears
Glue
Hole puncher

Step 1: Cut a piece of cardboard about 3 cm x 16 cm. Using pinking shears gives an attractive edge. Glue the flowers on the cardboard in a pretty spray.

Step 2: If the bookmark is a gift for someone, you can write their name at the bottom with gold or silver pen.

Step 3: Cut two pieces of clear plastic the same size as the cardboard and fasten one piece over the flowers, and the other over the back.

Step 4: Punch a hole at the top of the bookmark and loop a piece of cord or ribbon in it.

PRESSED FLOWER GREETING CARDS

Materials:

Pressed flowers
Coloured felt-tip pens
Varnish
Gold and silver felt-tip pens
Scissors
Thin coloured cardboard
Glitter
Glue
Coloured pencils

Step 1: Choose some cardboard to match your flowers. Cut out a rectangular piece and fold it in half. The card can be small or large, going lengthways or sideways.

Step 2: Rule a frame line around your card with a gold or silver pen. Now arrange the flowers and leaves attractively in the middle of your card.

Put a thin line of glue on the back of your dried plants and stick them onto your card.

Step 3: Cut out some thin white cardboard. On this draw something; perhaps some birds or flowers. Add touches of gold and silver pen to your pictures.

Glitter also looks nice on cards. You can stick it in the middle of flowers or just around the frame.

Step 4: If you draw something that you want shiny on your card, paint a coat of varnish over it. Eyes look really great varnished and if you draw a face and you want it to look as if the person is crying, trickle varnish down from the eyes for tears. Draw a frame on all of your cards to make them look good. If you find some spare wallpaper or pictures cut out the details which you like and stick them on a card. Go around them with silver and black felt-tip pen, and colour the background with pencils. Write birthday and festive greetings on your cards.

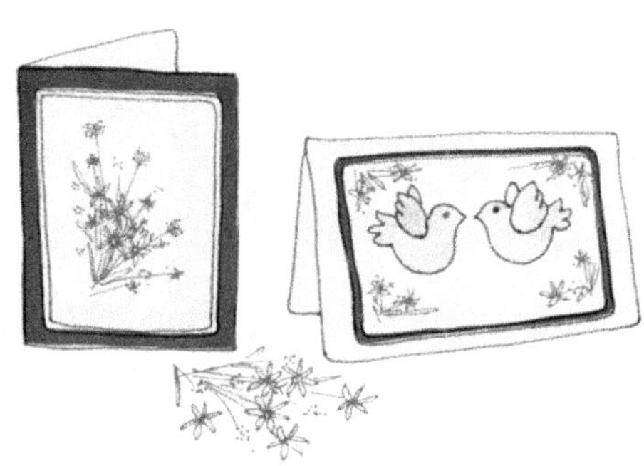

WRITING PAPER SETS

You can buy the coloured envelopes for these sets, or make your own.

Notepaper materials:

10 sheets thin coloured paper
1 gold felt-tip pen
Glue
Pressed flowers
Scissors
Coloured ribbon

Step 1: Cut out 10 pieces of coloured paper all the same size. The papers can be all one colour or mixed colours. Collect 10 different flowers and leaves and press them for three to four days by folding them between sheets of absorbent paper and placing heavy books on top of them.

Step 2: Arrange one flower or leaf on the top left corner of each paper. Handle the dried flowers carefully as they are very thin and brittle. Dribble a thin line of glue on the back of the pressed flowers and leaves and stick them onto the paper in the spot you want them.

Step 3: Set out the 10 coloured papers to dry. Once they have dried, rule a thin line around the edge with a gold pen. Leave a gap where the pressed flower is. You can make a writing paper set without the pressed flowers and just draw in little drawings like butterflies, birds and flowers with a thin gold pen.

Step 4: Place the 10 writing sheets together and 10 matching envelopes together too. Put the sheets on the bottom and envelopes on the top, and tie a ribbon around them to keep them together. Cut the loops on the bow and curl the ribbon's ends. If you like you can cover the writing paper set with clear cellophane for extra protection.

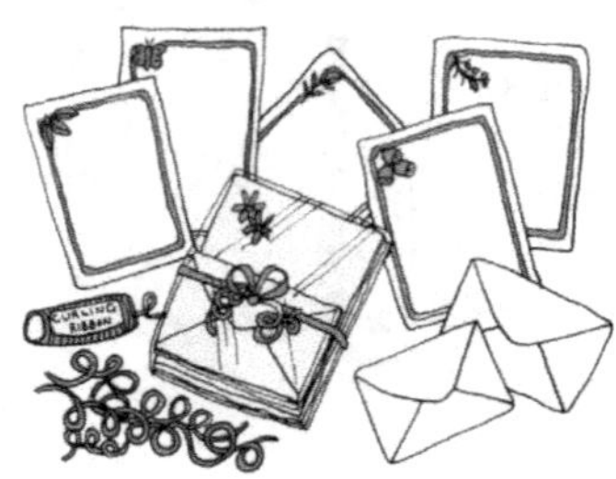

ENVELOPES

Materials:

10 sheets of coloured paper about 25 cm x *18 cm (or you can use printed gift-wrapping paper)*

Scissors

Glue

A plain sheet of white paper

Step 1: On the white paper, draw this pattern using the measurements shown, and cut it out along the solid lines. Dotted lines show where to make the folds. This is your template.

Step 2: Trace around the template onto the coloured papers and cut them out.

Step 3: Make folds 1, 2 and 3 as shown. Put a thin line of glue along each of the two flaps and fold your envelope together, pressing firmly. Make fold 4. Your envelope is ready.

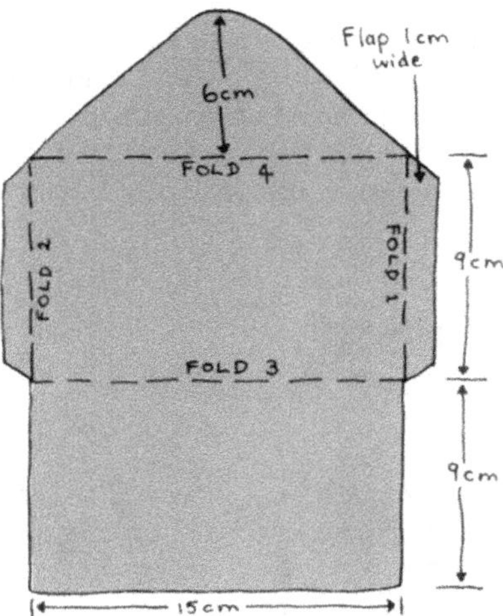

PRESSED FLOWER PICTURES

Materials:

A picture frame, small or large
A piece of heavy cardboard to fit inside frame
Printed gift paper or thin fabric
Tiny pressed flowers and leaves
Small scissors and tweezers
Glue and brush
Brown paper
Sticky tape

Step 1: Cut a piece of heavy cardboard to fit inside frame, unless it already has one. To make a pretty background for your pressed flowers cover the cardboard with the attractively printed paper or thin fabric. To do this, cut it the same size as the cardboard backing and fasten it on with glue.

Step 2: Choose the dried and pressed leaves you wish to use and, on a separate piece of paper, make them into a graceful design.

When you are satisfied with your design, transfer it piece by piece to the prepared background with tweezers. As you pick up each piece, brush the back of it with glue. I find it handy to put a puddle of glue in a saucer. Then I can draw a long piece, such as a stem, across it, or dip a paintbrush in it to paint the back of a piece with glue.

When the design is glued to the background, cover it with a piece of glass that fits the frame, and place both inside the frame. Now cut a piece of brown wrapping paper to fit the back of the frame, and fasten it to it with tape or glue. This will not only hide the backing, but will also keep out dust and moisture.

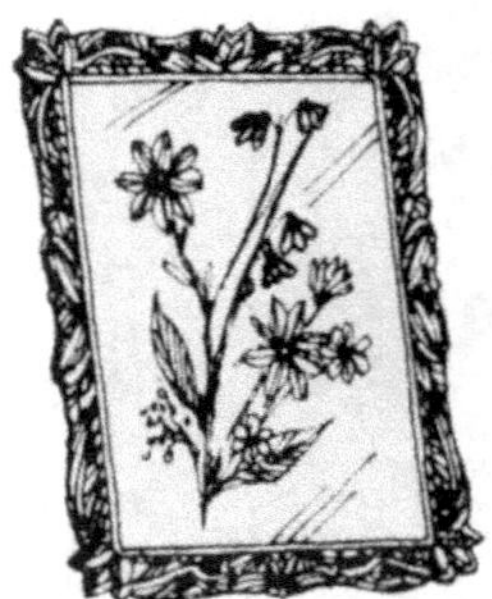

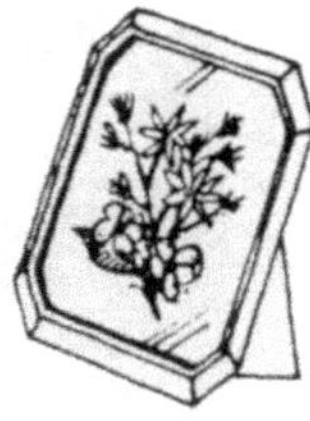

POLYMER AND AIR-DRY MODELLING CLAY

Modelling clay is a compound that stays soft until you harden it by baking (polymer clay) or air-drying (air-dry clay). When using modelling clay you first have to soften it. This can be done by breaking off small pieces and kneading them with your fingers. It can be bought at toy or craft shops, and is available in many different colours.

Polymer Clay

Polymer clay can be hardened by baking at a low temperature in the home oven. There are several brands available—FIMO and Sculpey, for example.

Follow the baking instructions on the packet. Polymer clay objects are usually placed on a foil-lined tray and baked in an oven preheated to 100° C (275° F). They take between ten and twenty minutes to harden. As soon as there is a slight smell, turn the oven off to prevent overbaking. Leave the models to cool before painting, glueing or varnishing.

Polymer Clay: Advantages

- A wide range of colors available.
- You can also buy sparkly and shiny clays.
- Your model does not shrink when the clay hardens.

Polymer Clay: Disdvantages

- Young children should not use hot ovens. Oven-baked clay is suitable only for children aged 8 years or more.
- An adult must supervise the baking.
- How well your model turns out will depend on how long you bake it and the different thicknesses of material in your model.
- If you wish to glue or paint your hardened model you may need to buy special glues and paints.
- Polymer clay usually costs more than air-dry clay.

Air-dry Clay

Air-dry clays (sometimes called 'ADC') gradually go hard at room temperature without needing any baking. The drying and hardening takes between 24 hours to several days, depending on how big the model is and whether the weather is hot or cold.

Crayola Model Clay and Amaco Cloud Clay are good for use by young children, ideally 2 years old and above. These brands are easy to handle, mess-free and non-toxic.

Makin's clay dries hard and is excellent for older children who like making figurines, jewellery and ornaments.

Air-dry Clay: Advantages

- Easy to work with, and can be used by very young children.
- Ordinary glues, paints and varnishes can be applied to finished models.
- Air-dry clays generally cost less than polymer clays.

Air-dry Clay: Disadvantages

- The clay loses moisture when it dries, so your model will shrink approximately 5-15% as it hardens.
- It takes longer to air-dry large models than it would to oven-bake them.
- Air-dried modeling compounds are not suitable for making vessels that will contain liquids, such as cups or bowls.

VICTORIAN SALT CLAY

Salt ceramic, also called Victorian salt clay is an air-dry modeling clay that can be made in the kitchen. Salt ceramic dries to a coarse, stone-like texture, and so is often used in folk craft and children's art. Like other air-dried modelling compounds, it is not suitable for vessels that will contain liquids. Popular uses of salt ceramic include making jewellery and Christmas ornaments. In jewellery making, it can be rolled into balls and formed into beads, or pressed into various shapes. In making Christmas ornaments it is sometimes made into balls, similar to the bead-making process, or rolled out with a rolling pin and cut with cookie cutters and painted.

It takes about two days for the objects to dry. Victorian Salt Clay takes paint well, once hardened. People often coat it with acrylic, once hardened, to protect it from moisture.[1]

The following recipe should be made by an adult, for children to use.

Recipe

2 cups salt
⅔ cup water and ½ cup cold water
1 cup cornstarch

- Mix salt and ⅔ cup water in a pan. Stirring constantly, heat over a low flame for about 4 minutes but do not allow it to boil. Remove from heat.
- Quickly mix cornstarch and ½ cup cold water together and add this combination in one go to heated mixture.
- Stir and mix quickly. If resulting mixture is not a thick paste, place back on low heat and stir for about a minute until mixture stiffens to a dough-like consistency.
- Place salt clay on wax paper to cool, covered with a damp cloth.
- Knead clay like bread dough on flat surface until dough is a smooth and pliable mass. Can be stored in plastic or foil and kept in an airtight container.

Colouring the Salt Clay

1 *Source: Wikipedia, "Salt Ceramic'. Article retrieved 12th May 2015.*

The clay is naturally white. Color, such as food colouring or paint, can be added when dough is being cooked or when it is being kneaded, or modeled objects can be painted when dry.

Drying the Salt Clay

It takes 2 days for a modeled object to dry at room temperature.

For quicker results, preheat oven to 175° C (350° F), and then turn the oven off. Put the model in the oven, preferably on a wire rack, and leave it there until the oven has cooled down.

Finishing Salt Clay Models

You can smooth dry models by rubbing them gently with sandpaper or an emery board.

Using Salt Clay

Wrap unused pices of salt clay in aluminum foil while you work, to keep them soft.

When shaping this clay, line your work surfaces with wax paper to stop things from getting too sticky.

After salt clay has dried it can be painted with acrylics, watercolors or tempera paints.

Coat dried and painted models with varnish, or with a mixture of half white craft glue and half water to seal them from moisture.

Helpful Hints

To make beads for a necklace, punch holes with a toothpick while the clay is still pliable. You can also string the beads through a thin wire, letting them dry on the wire itself.

Salt clay can also be rolled out like cookie dough and cut with a cookie cutter.

Note: 'Mastic cold porcelain', also known as 'kitchen craft clay', uses bicarbonate of soda rather than salt. It is preferred by people who dislike working with salt. Take ¼ cup of water, ¼cup of cornstarch and ¼ cup of bicarb soda. Mix all ingredients together and cook (stirring) until it forms a ball.

MODELLING CLAY WALL PLAQUES

Before you make wall plaques, collect all sorts of tiny sparkly things — sequins, tiny beads, pearls, stars, fake jewellery. They make great decorations.

Note: The colours that are named in these projects can be changed around and look just as effective.

CLOWN WALL PLAQUE

Materials:

Modelling clay
Beads
Hook
Sequins

Step 1: To make a clown wall plaque, roll out a flat oval for the base. Place a thin pink circle in the centre of the oval for a head. Roll two thin black crosses with a bead in the middle for eyes. Put a red diamond or ball for the nose. For the mouth roll a red stripe in a smile, with a line through the middle. Make a pointy hat and a bit of brown hair on both sides.

Step 2: Make a shape to fill in the shoulders and neck. Put two small red sequins for the cheeks. Around the edge, place small beads for a frame. Stick on a hook for hanging.

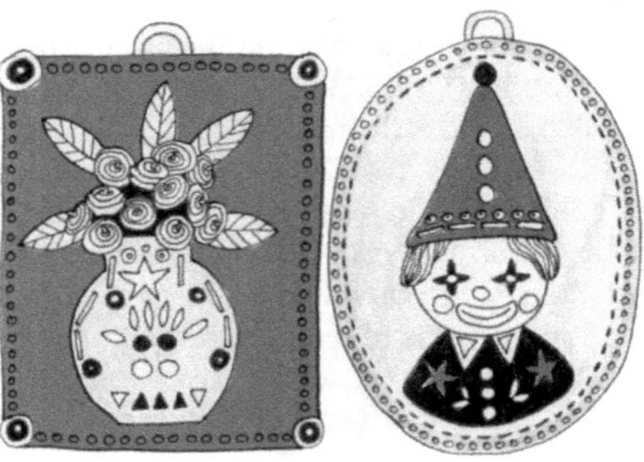

VASE OF FLOWERS WALL PLAQUE

Materials:

Modelling clay
Assorted small beads
One toothpick
Hook

Step 1: Roll out some orange modelling clay. With a knife cut it into a rectangle. Then roll out some purple modelling clay very thinly and cut it out into the shape of a vase. Stick it on the bottom of the rectangle, right way up. To make flowers, roll thin strips of lilac, red and pink modelling clay; flatten them out and roll them up in a spiral flower shape.

Step 2: Stick the flowers on the top of the vase. You do not need anything like glue or water to stick modelling clay; if you press it, it sticks by itself.

Roll out tiny, thin rolls of colours of modelling clay and press them into the middle of each flower, for a daffodil effect. Then cut out some thin green leaves and arrange them around the flowers. Press small glass beads around the edge of the rectangular wall plaque. Attach four small purple dots on each corner. Add a hook to hang it up.

NAME WALL PLAQUE

Use a thin roll of modelling clay to write with. Name wall plaques can be used to decorate bedroom doors and they make a good gift.

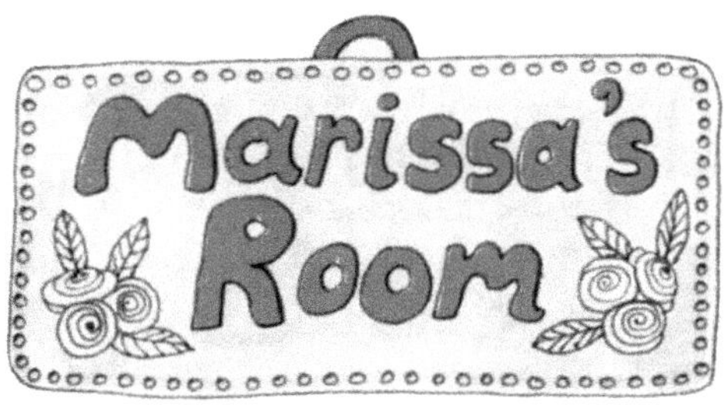

MODELLING CLAY EARRINGS

When you are making earrings make sure the colours go together e.g. pink and purple look good, whilst brown and green isn't as effective.

Also think of contrast. It looks good if you make a shape which is a strong colour, and the same shape in the middle, which is smaller, from another colour.

Materials:

Modelling clay
Fake diamonds
Foil
Tiny glass beads
Stud pins with backings[1]
Varnish

Step 1: To make marble effect studs, you choose the colours you will use, then roll every separate colour into a thin stripe. Twist the stripes into a worm and knead them together

Step 2: Once you have done this, make some flat shapes — circles, squares, triangles, love hearts etc. Make sure at least one side has a perfectly flat surface, as you will be sticking it onto a stud pin. If you want a pattern on your shapes, with something sharp, draw lines or spots. Arrange shapes onto a foiled tray.

Step 3: To make sparkly earrings press a diamond into the middle of your shape. If your shape is long, press a few diamonds in. Diamonds look good in any colour, not just clear. Arrange some tiny glass beads around the diamonds. In the oven the diamonds and beads will not melt.

Step 4: Set all your earrings on a foiled tray to bake them. Once cooked, leave the shapes to cool and glaze with varnish or clear nail polish. Turn the earring upside down and with very strong glue, stick the pin onto the back base. Then thread on the backing.

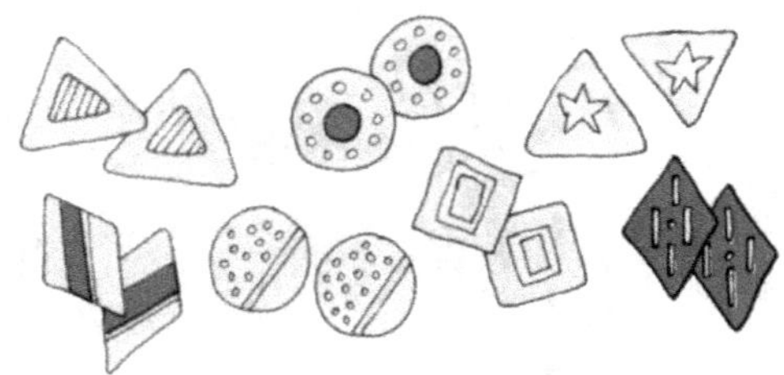

1 *These stud pins are available from craft shops.*

LEAF AND SEEDPOD NECKLACES

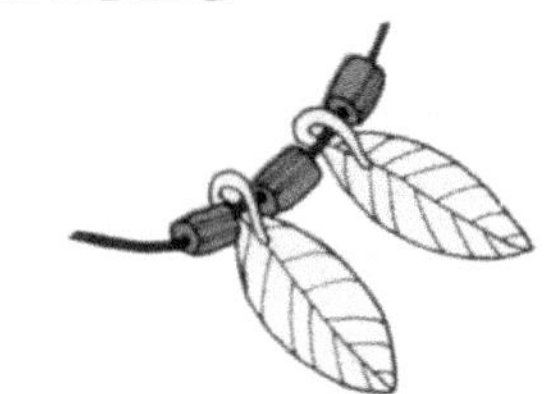

Materials:

Polymer modelling clay
90 cm leather string
Toothpicks
A metal skewer

Step 1: To make the leaves, you have two choices. You can either roll modelling clay out flat and cut a leaf shape out with a knife, or you can roll a ball, mould and flatten a leaf shape with your hands. I find the second choice is neater because the edge isn't as rough.

Step 2: Note that just because you are making leaves, they don't have to be green. In fact they look good pink, red or lilac. For a different effect, marble the modelling clay with two colours (e.g. white and pink) and make leaves out of that. (See earring instructions for marbling.)

Once you have your leaf shape, poke two holes side by side on the top of your leaf with a skewer. This is so you can later thread the leather through. Alternatively you can make a long leaf stem and curve it over to make a loop. Engrave the lines on the leaf with a toothpick or skewer.

Step 3: Roll three tiny balls and stick them together on the top corner of the leaf, near the holes. With a toothpick, poke holes in the centre of the tiny balls. These represent seedpods. Make five leaves the same colour. On these you can make all the seedpods the same colour or make one leaf with red, one white, one red etc.

Step 4: Make six beads. They should be the same colour as the seedpods. Make beads by rolling balls and threading them onto a metal skewer. You can choose the colours on your necklace to match your favourite clothes.

Step 5: Bake leaves on foil, face up. Leave the skewer in when cooking the beads. Once cooked, you can either varnish them or just leave them plain. Thread them on leather — bead, leaf, bead, leaf etc. At the end of both beads, tie a knot so they stay on.

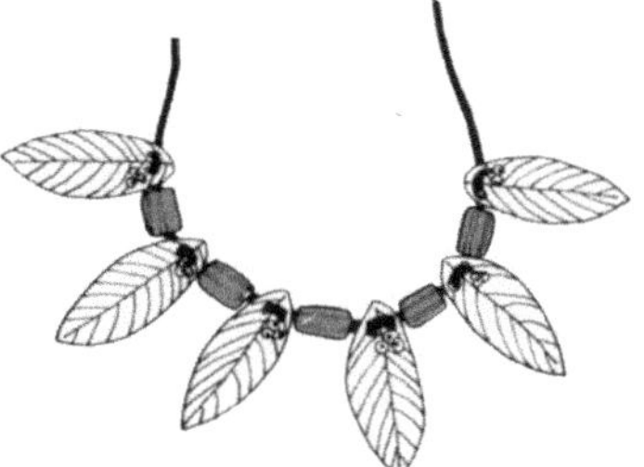

FLOWER NECKLACES

Materials:

modelling clay
A toothpick
90 cm leather string (1 necklace)
A metal skewer

Step 1: To make a flower necklace you need three colours of modelling clay. Turquoise, red and pink look good together. Make a roll with turquoise modelling clay. Cut the roll into six even pieces with a knife. Roll every piece into a ball and flatten them out into an oval. Join these petals together to make a daisy.

Step 2: In the middle of the flower put a small light pink ball and flatten it. In the middle of that, place a smaller red flat ball. On each petal, with a toothpick engrave two small dashes. Carefully put the daisy face down. Make a short thin roll. Place a skewer lightly over the back of the flower and use it as a base to stick the roll on. See diagram. This hook is to thread the flowers on the leather.

Step 3: Make three daisies, 3 to 4 cm wide. Then make eight small red beads and eight small pale pink beads.

Cook them and thread them onto the leather as shown. Put on the beads — one pink, one red, one pink etc.

Step 4: Now to make the lily necklace. Cut out a white semi circle about 6 cm wide, 3 cm high. Curl it from the centre so that the two corners are roughly on top of each other. You can practise and trace with a piece of paper. Make a long yellow roll and put it down the centre of the lily.

Step 5: Make eight very small white beads and eight very small yellow beads. With green modelling clay make four green leaves. Cook them. On the top of your lilies and leaves, glue a little hook to hang with. Thread them on as shown on the diagram.

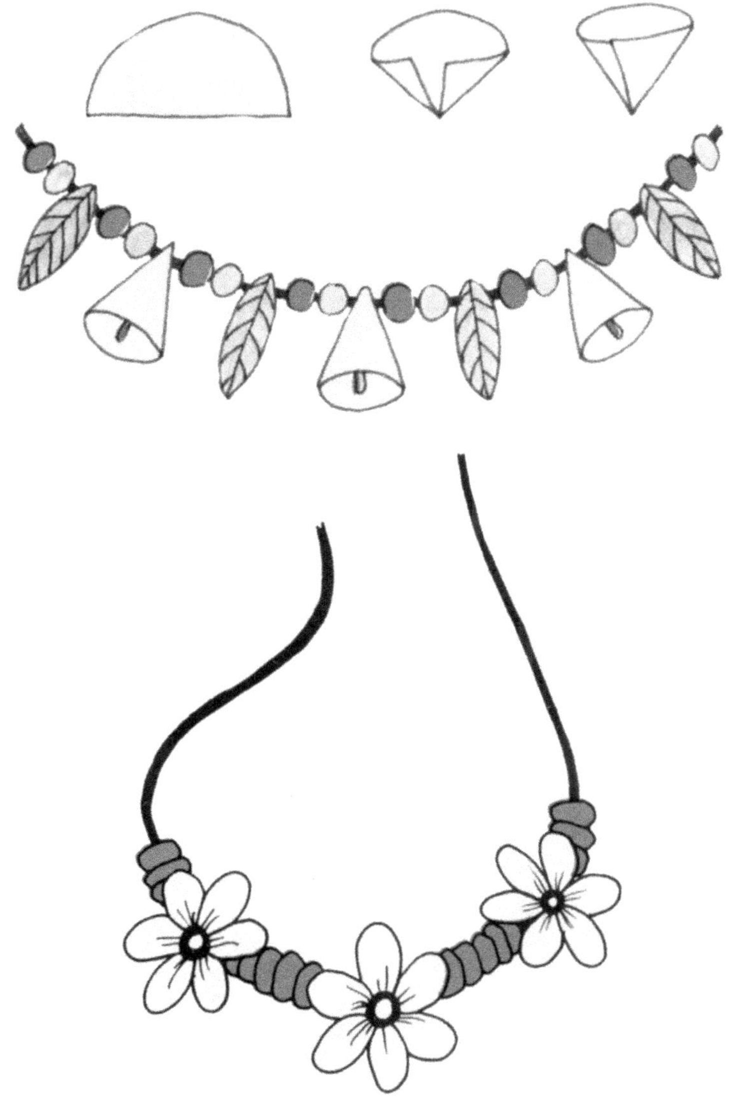

NATURE CRAFTS

The next time you go for a walk or a bicycle ride, particularly in the countryside or parkland, be on the lookout for anything unusual or beautiful that you may never have noticed before. It may be a pretty seedpod or an attractive bunch of dried grass, a piece of twisted wood or a pine cone, an unusual leaf or pebble, or a shell.

Keep a collection of these natural materials at home. There are many imaginative ways you can use them for creative projects.

POMANDER BALL

Pomander balls are easy to make and people love to receive them as gifts. They can be hung in wardrobes and linen cupboards to make clothes smell sweet and spicy.

Materials:

An orange

A packet of whole cloves

A meat skewer or a long sharp nail

Some ribbon

Use the sharp end of the skewer to puncture the skin of the orange so that you can push cloves into the rind. Stick the cloves close together in circles around the orange until the whole surface is entirely covered. Now push the skewer or nail through the centre of the orange, and tie a ribbon bow to it at each end. If the pomander ball is to be hung, make a long loop of the ribbon to hang it by.

The orange will shrivel and dry, the oil of its skin blending with the spiciness of the cloves to give a wonderful fragrance.

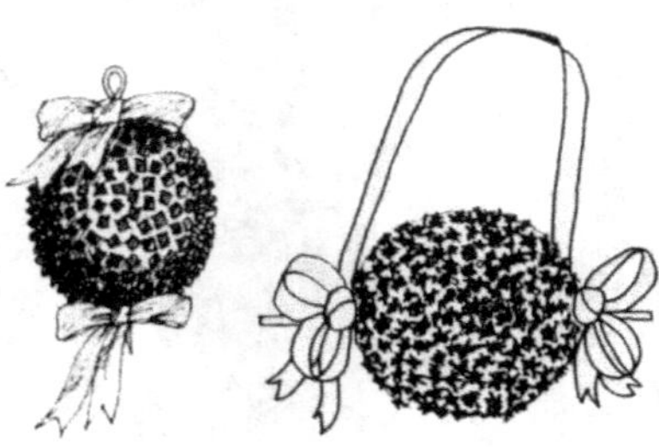

DECORATED BASKET LIDS

Materials:

Strong glue
Tiny leaves
Varnish
Green acrylic paint
Gumnuts (large and small)
Acorn shells
Small cane baskets with lids

Step 1: Collect large gumnuts, small gumnuts, acorns etc. Then arrange them nicely on the top of the cane lid.

Step 2: Make sure your arrangement is in the centre of the lid. With some strong glue, stick some acorn shells and small and large gumnuts in the middle, with three or four leaves facing outwards. If you are not satisfied with the arrangement, you can change it around while the glue is still wet.

Step 3: So that the leaves don't go brown, mix up a green paint the same colour as the leaves and put a thin coat of paint over them. Make sure the leaves are stuck down properly so that they don't curl up. When dry, varnish the whole design.

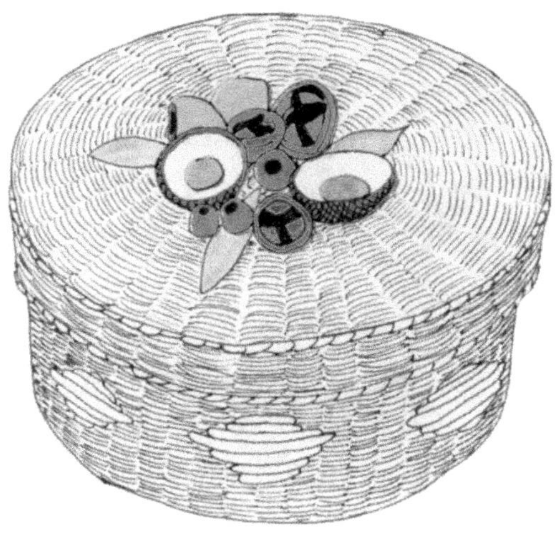

POTPOURRI

Another sweet-smelling gift you can make is potpourri. This is a mixture of dried flower petals and it too is used to make wardrobes and chests of drawers fresh.

Gather the petals of any sweet-smelling flowers that are in full bloom but not past their prime. Gather them on a day when it hasn't rained for twenty-four hours. There are many that you can use — mock orange, lilac, orange blossoms, oleander, violets, carnations, pinks, heliotrope, verbena, acacia and, most important of all, roses. Try to have at least four times as many rose petals as all the others. In addition to flower petals, it is nice to have the leaves of herbs, like rosemary, thyme, mint, bay leaf, rose geranium and lemon verbena.

You can dry the petals and leaves on any flat surface, but if you have an old window screen or a piece of coarse cheesecloth that you can stretch between two chairs it would be better, for then the air can circulate around them.

When the petals are thoroughly dry, mix them together and package them. If the potpourri is to go on a shelf you can package it in little jars, such as baby-food jars or small mayonnaise jars. If it is for a chest of drawers, a pretty way to package it is to put a square of thin, coloured cloth about five inches square on top of a square of nylon net the same size. Put a mound of potpourri on the cloth and draw the cloth and net up around it, tying it with a ribbon.

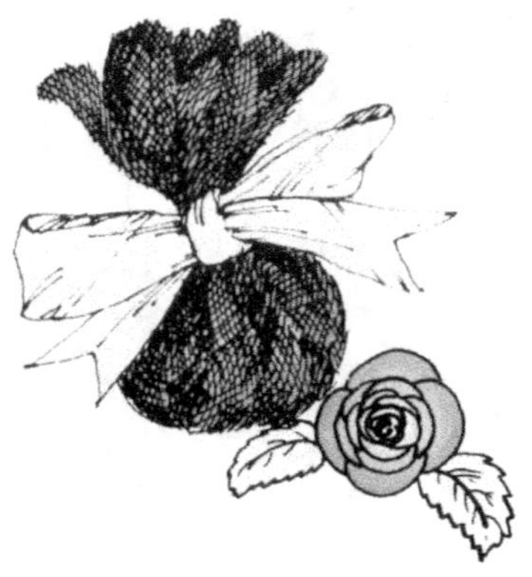

GUMNUT DOGS

Materials:

Large gumnuts[2]
Red felt
Paint
Strong glue
Varnish
Very tiny gumnuts

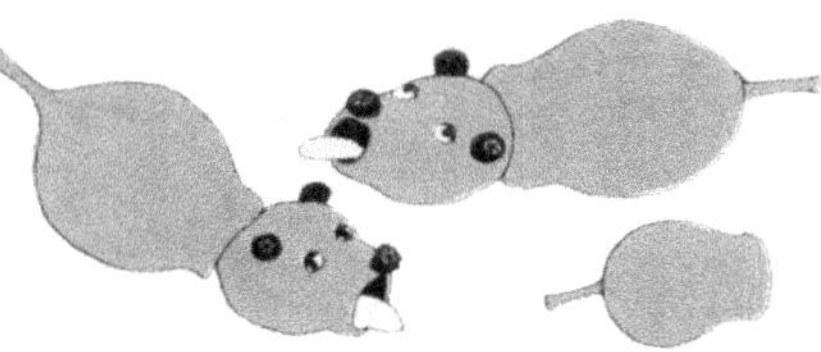

Step 1: Go for a nature walk and collect large and smaller gumnuts. You can find very tiny roundish gumnuts for the ears and nose on bushes and trees. These should be ½ cm long.

The next step is to match them up. This means getting a little gumnut and a large gumnut and fitting the smaller one into the hole of the larger one. If it doesn't fit well and there is a noticeable gap, try another gumnut.

Step 2: Once you have fitted the gumnuts, put a thin line of glue around the edge of the hole in the large gumnut. Fit the smaller gumnut into the larger one. The two gumnut holes should be facing the same direction. Leave the stem on the large gumnut for a tail.

Step 3: Once the glue has dried, the next step is to paint it. You can use just about any paint including acrylic and undiluted water colour. Paint on thin brown, white, black or grey strokes to give the effect of "fur".

Instead of painting fur, you could paint on white and black spots. Only paint the fur or the spots on the larger gumnut (the body). On the small gumnut, paint two white dots for eyes, with two smaller black dots in the centre for pupils. Then paint some black eyebrows.

Step 4: Paint three tiny gumnuts black; because they are so small, it is easier to just put black paint on your fingertips and rub it on the gumnuts. Two are for the ears, which are stuck roughly above the two eyebrows. The other one is for the nose, stuck on the rim of the small gumnut, between the eyes.

Step 5: Cut out a small tongue out of red felt and glue it into the opening hole with a bit sticking out. This makes it look like the dog is panting. Give this a nice finish by applying two coats of varnish.

2 *Gumnuts are the seeds of some eucalyptus trees.*

AUTUMN LEAF MOBILE

Materials:

Assorted pressed autumn leaves
A piece of twisty wood with lots of ends
or
An attractive coathanger
Strong thread or fishing line
Craft glue which is transparent when dry
Paintbrush

Step 1: Suspend the twisty wood or the coathanger from a piece of thread.

Step 2: Spread the leaves out on paper. Cut pieces of thread in different lengths. The leaves will hang from the pieces of thread.

Step 3: Now paint a thin coat of craft glue on the surface of each leaf, making sure the entire leaf is covered. Put an end of thread at the top of each leaf and fasten it there with the glue.

Step 4: On these threads of different lengths, fasten the leaves to the twisty wood or the coathanger. They are very pretty as they float about. In summer, you could make a shell mobile instead.

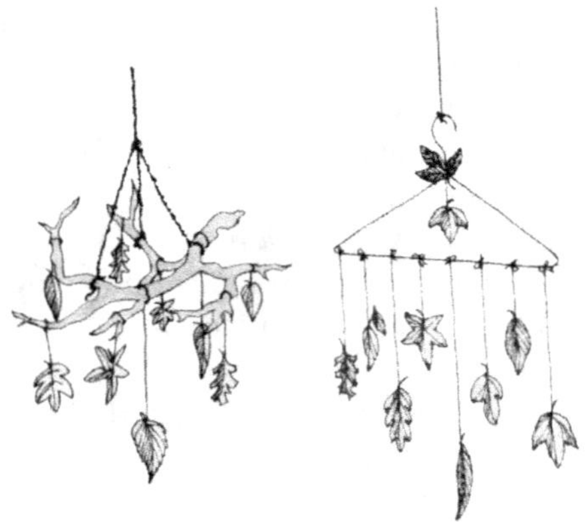

SEED MOSAICS

Materials:

Varnish
Black felt tip pen
Brush
Tweezers
Backing
Glue
Seeds

Mosaic seed work is useful in decorating wooden boxes, jars, cork mats and matchboxes, as well as making wall plaques. Mosaics are made by glueing a variety of seeds and dried beans close together in a pattern, until the whole surface is covered.

There are so many seeds, and they come in so many different sizes, shapes, and colours that they are convenient to use in making mosaic pictures.

There are green and yellow dried peas; popping corn; peppercorns; rice; speckled butter beans; baby lima beans; melon; pumpkin; squash and grapefruit seeds; pinto beans; kidney beans; sunflower seeds; coffee beans; pepper berries and mixed birdseed. All these and many more can be used for mosaic work.

It is fun to make mosaics in a group, because then you can share a mutual supply of materials.

A Mosaic Picture

For a mosaic picture you can use a background of heavy cardboard, plywood, cork, thin wood or similar material.

Draw a design on the background. A simple, bold design is the most successful. You might do a picture of a fish for someone's bathroom, or a nursery-rhyme figure such as Humpty Dumpty for a child's bedroom, or an intricate geometric design.

Divide the design into sections according to the colours you want to use and then choose seeds of the proper colour and shape for each section. Usually you use just one kind of seed in each section. In effect, you will be "painting" with seeds.

Work on one section at a time. Paint each section with glue, then place the seeds in it with tweezers, covering the surface of each section solidly. When the design is finished, completely fill in the surrounding area with seeds that will make a good background for the picture. When dry, spray or paint the whole picture with varnish.

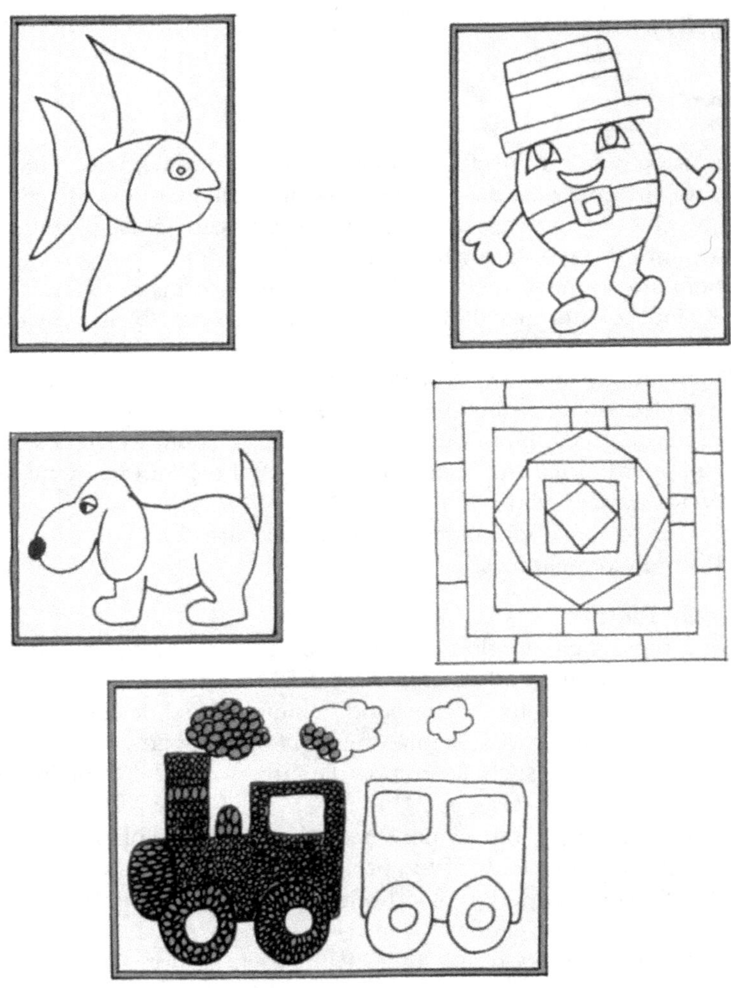

HOW TO DRY FLOWERS

You can make a beautiful bouquet of dried flowers that look so fresh you will have to touch them to realise they have not just been picked. They will last for months.

Materials:

A small box with a lid, e.g. a shoe box
Two cups of powdered Borax
One cup of sifted dry sand (salt free)
Florists' wire
Flowers
Soft paintbrush

Note:

1. You may have to double or triple the amount of Borax and sand in order to make enough mixture to cover your flowers completely.
2. If the flowers are left too long in this mixture, some of the colours will fade. You can use plain sand without the Borax; it takes a bit longer for the flowers to dry but it preserves the colours well. Sand must be very dry and washed free of all salt.

Step 1: Make sure flowers are dry when you pick them. Cut off the natural stem about 2 cm below the flower head and replace it with a wire. Run the wire through the centre of the flower.

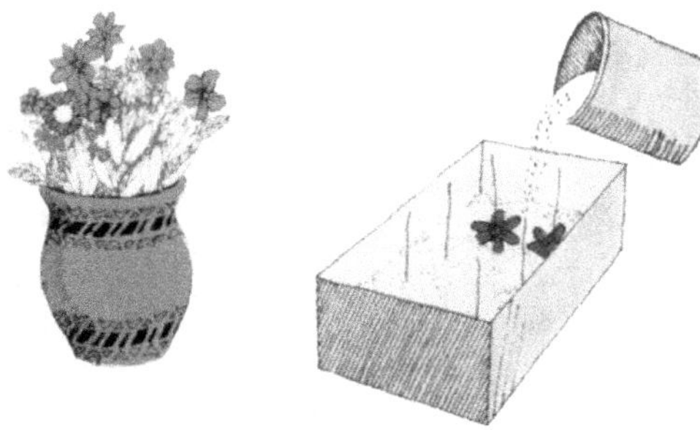

Step 2: Put 2 cm of sand mixture in the box. Place flat flowers like daisies and zinnias face down on it, with the wire sticking straight up. Be sure to leave a little space between each flower.

Step 3: Then carefully sift more of the sand mixture over and around each flower until it is thoroughly covered to a depth of 2 cm.

Step 4: Place many-petalled flowers like dahlias, roses or asters face up, bending the wire stems so that the flowers will be straight, and gently sift the sand between the petals until the flower is covered to a depth of 2 cm.

Step 5: Tightly cover the box and write the date on the lid. The flowers will take two or three weeks to dry, depending on the type of flower and whether you have mixed Borax with the sand.

Step 6: When you think the flowers are dry, carefully brush the sand from one flower with a soft paintbrush. If it is properly dried it should have the texture of stiff silk.

HOW TO PRESERVE LEAVES

At the same time you are drying the flowers you can prepare foliage to use in the bouquet.

This is done by simply standing branches of leaves in a mixture of ⅓ glycerin and ⅔ water. The glycerin is absorbed through the stem and preserves the leaves indefinitely.

A leaf, which takes about the same time as a flower, is ready when tiny drops of moisture appear on it, and it may turn from green to an attractive shade of brown or bronze.

You can buy glycerin in pharmacies, drugstores and supermarkets.

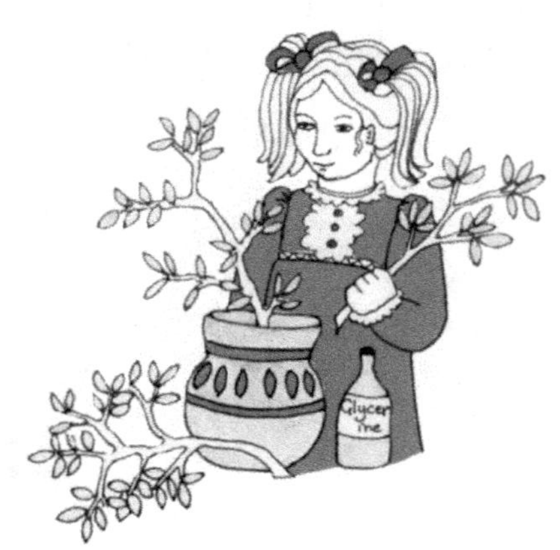

PAPIER MACHE

Papier mache can be used in two forms: *pulp* and *strip*. For both forms you will need lots of newspaper and glue. The glue can be either wallpaper paste, which is readily available from paint and hardware shops, or homemade glue. For home-made glue, mix two cups of plain flour and a pinch of salt with enough water to make it gooey and sticky but not runny.

PAPIER MACHE NECKLACE

Materials:

Fishing line
Absorbent white paper
Skewer or toothpicks
Paint
Glue
Fabric (netting or old panty hose)
Varnish

Step 1: This necklace is made using the pulp method. Tear several sheets of paper into pieces approximately 2 or 3 cm. (1 to 1 ½ in.) in diameter.

Step 2: Soak the pieces in a bowl of water for several hours or overnight.

Step 3: Squeeze the water out of the paper or drain it through a piece of open-weave fabric such as netting, muslin or old panty hose.

Step 4: Put the soggy paper into a bowl and gradually add glue, mixing well with your hands, until the mixture feels like clay.

Step 5: Form large and small beads. They can be round, elongated or cube-shaped. Pierce each bead with a toothpick or skewer and allow the beads to dry. This can take a few days.

Step 6: When dry, paint the beads in bright colours, varnish them and thread them onto the fishing line in an attractive pattern, e.g. one large, two small, alternating.

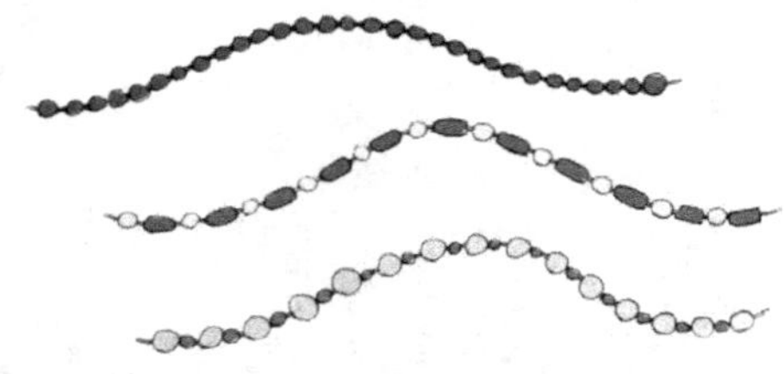

PAPIER MACHE BOTTLE DOLL

Materials:

An attractively shaped bottle, (e.g. a "Mateus Rose" wine bottle)
Absorbent white paper

Newspaper	*Glue (home-made or wallpaper paste)*
Paint	*Paintbrush*
Aluminium foil	*Small dried flowers*
Varnish	*Twisted yarn for hair*

The doll is made using the papier mache 'strip' method and some 'pulp'.

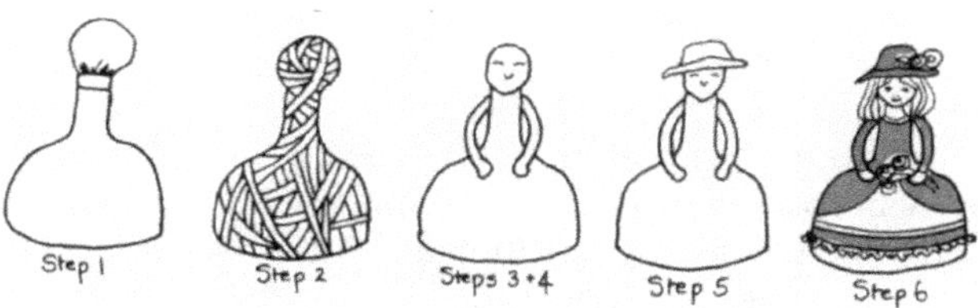

Step 1: Make the head by crushing a wad of newspaper to the size you want, covering it with foil to keep the shape and stuffing it into the top of the bottle.

Step 2: Now tear the newspaper into lots of strips about 1 or 2 cm (½ to 1 inch) wide. Soak each strip in glue and cover the entire bottle and head with at least three layers of strips, smoothing the strips down well.

Step 3: When dry, cover everything with strips of white paper soaked in glue. Then, using the white paper, build up a face on the head. The eyebrows will overhang the eye sockets slightly. Cheeks are rounded. Stick on a straight nose, lips and a chin. The face is easier to make if you use tiny scraps of paper well soaked in glue to form a clay-like pulp.

Step 4: Form arms and hands from white paper and stick them on.

Step 5: A hat can be made from thin cardboard and gluey white paper strips. Allow the doll to a few days to get completely dry.

Step 6: Paint the face, arms, body, dress and hat. Varnish, then glue on hanks of yarns for hair, and flowers on the hat and in her hand.

BIG PIG MONEY BOX

Materials:

A balloon
Newspaper
Cardboard egg carton
Paint
Scissors
Glue (home-made or wallpaper)
Pipecleaner
Varnish
Absorbent white paper

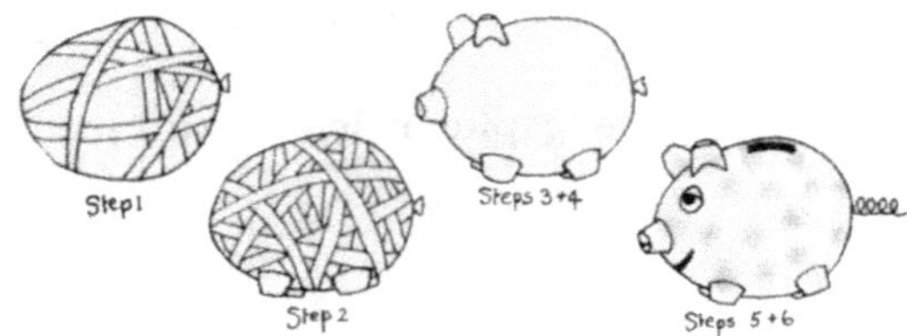

Step 1: Blow up the balloon to the size you want and tie the end. Cover the balloon with lots of layers of newspaper strips 1 or 2 cm (½ to 1 inch) wide soaked in glue, leaving only the tied end of the balloon sticking out. You may need to build up these layers over two or three days, allowing to dry overnight. The papier mache will dry more quickly if you leave it near a heater.

Step 2: When the layers are thick enough to make a strong shell (about ¾ cm or ⅓ inch), tear up some strips of white paper and soak them in glue. Cut off four 'cups' from the egg carton and stick them on with white paper strips for the four little feet. Make sure your pig can stand up!

Step 3: Another 'cup' forms the pig's nose. Glue it on at the opposite end from the tied end of the balloon, which should be still sticking out.

Step 4: Cut another 'cup' into two halves, which form the two ears. Stick them on with white strips and cover the whole pig with a layer of white.

Step 5: When the pig is completely dry and hard, hold onto the end of the balloon, burst it, and pull it out through the tail. Paint your pig with a design of spots or flowers, not forgetting two big eyes, a mouth and two nostrils.

Step 6: Paint a pipecleaner, twist it into a spiral and glue it into the hole for the tail. Varnish the pig and with a sharp knife (get an adult to help) cut a slot in its back for the money.

PAPIER MACHE CONTAINER

Materials:

A plastic container (e.g. an ice-cream or margarine container)
Strips of newspaper *Glue (home-made or wallpaper)*
White paper *Paint*
Varnish

This pretty container can be used for crayons, pencils or odds and ends.

Step 1: Wet the outside of the plastic container with plain water and cover it completely with strips of newspaper, smoothing them down.

Step 2: Now build up several layers of strips soaked in glue. Continue until this shell is about ¾ cm (⅓ inch) thick.

Step 3: Cover the shell with white paper strips, smoothed down well. Allow the container to begin to dry, so that it becomes strong.

Step 4: Before the papier mache is completely dry and hard, gently manoeuvre the plastic container out from inside it. You may need to insert a thin knife between the inner and outer containers, to loosen them.

Step 5: Line the inside of your papier mache container with white paper. Use more paper to make the top edge smooth. Allow to dry completely, then paint in bright colours and coat with clear, glossy varnish.

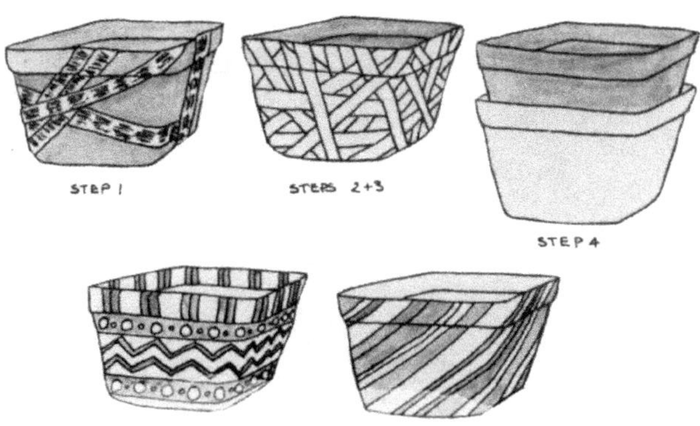

ODDS AND ENDS

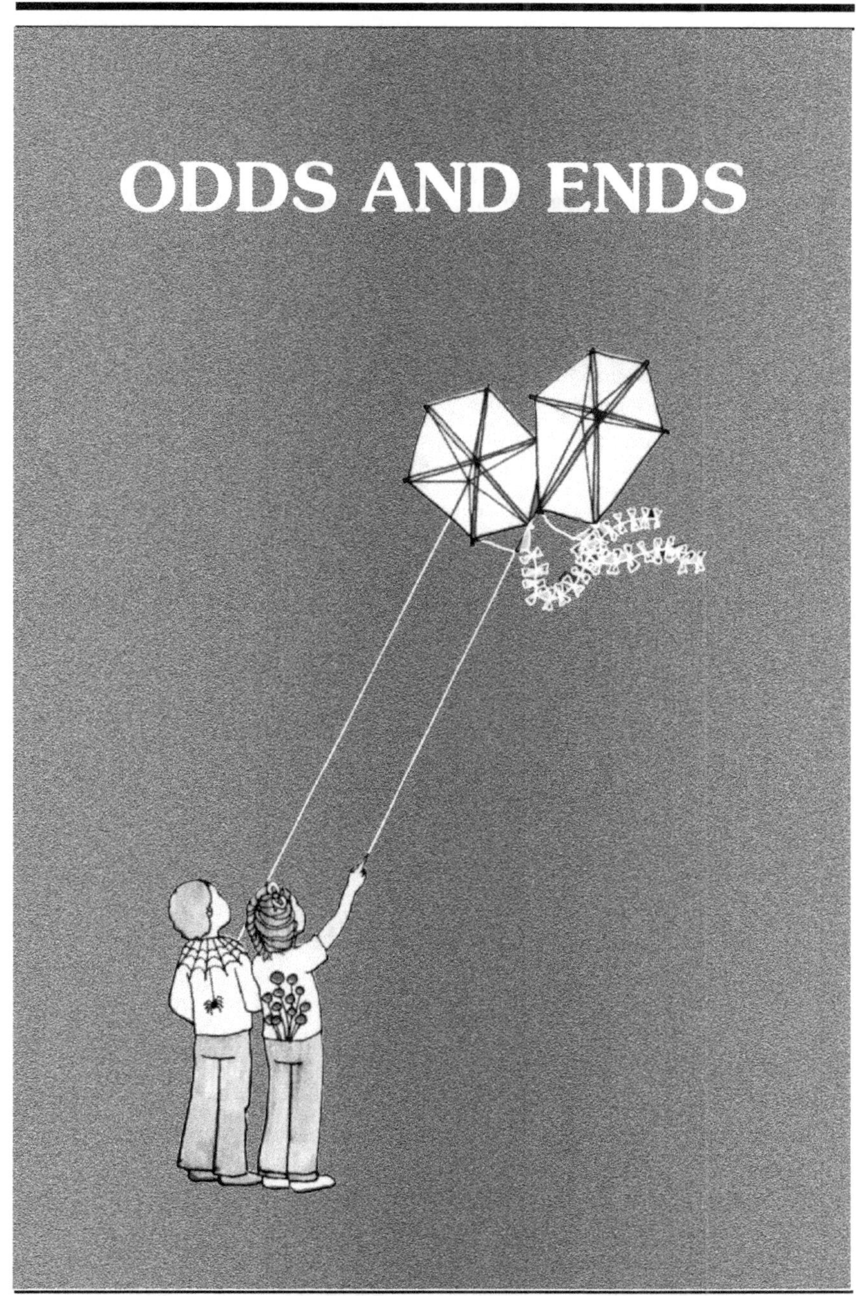

THREE-STICK KITE

Materials:

Three dowels about 1 cm wide, or three thin wooden sticks
Newspaper or some other thin paper for covering

Scissors	*String*
Strong glue	*Scraps of cloth*

Note: Two of the dowels should be 90 cm (35 inches) long and one should be 75 cm (30 inches) long.

Step 1: Cross the dowels as shown in the diagram and tie them tightly together at the centre joint, adding glue for extra strength.

Step 2: Cut a notch in both ends of each stick and stretch string between the notches to outline the shape of the kite. Wrap string around the ends of the sticks to keep them from splitting.

Step 3: Lay this frame on the paper and draw an outline 4 cm (1 ½inches) bigger than the frame. Cut this out.

Step 4: Fold the paper over the string and glue it in place.

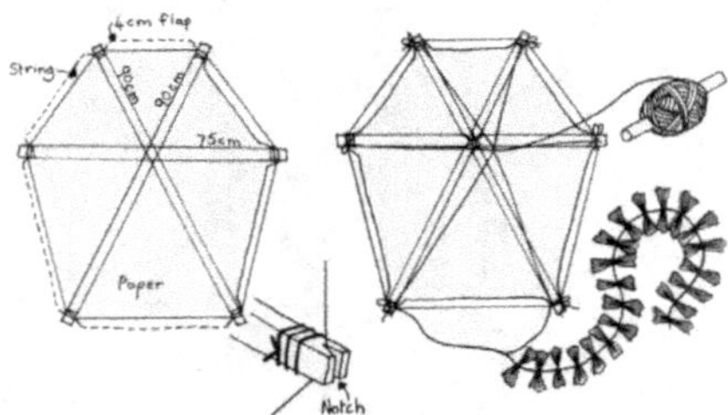

Step 5: Take three lengths of string and fasten each one from one end of each stick to the other end. At the point where these three strings cross, tie one end of a ball of string for flying the kite.

Step 6: For a tail, tie a length of string between the ends of the two long sticks and at the centre point of this length, fasten a 90 cm string to which short cloth strips have been tied.

If you have used white paper, you can paint an attractive design on your kite.

DECORATED T-SHIRTS

Fabric painting is useful for decorating T-shirts, windcheaters, jeans, hankies, tablecloths and pillowcases. You can buy the paints from craft and toy stores. Special crayons for drawing on fabric are also available — these are less messy than paints. Or you can simply use felt-tip pens.

Follow the instructions on the paints or crayons. After the articles have been painted, sew on pompoms, buttons, tassels, feather, beads or sequins for added effect. Here are some designs you could use for T-shirts.

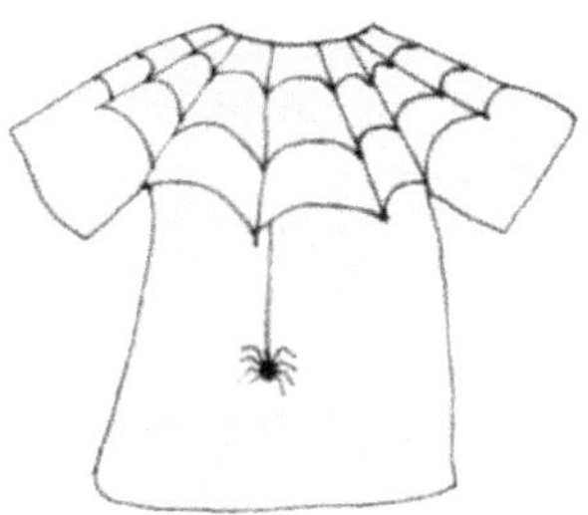

Spider T-shirt

Use black crayon on a white or coloured T-shirt.

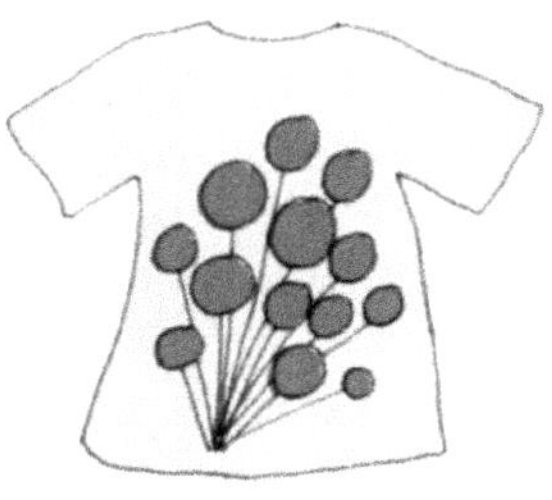

Balloon T-shirt

Outline the balloons in black or dark red and colour them with bright shades of blue, pink, green and yellow.

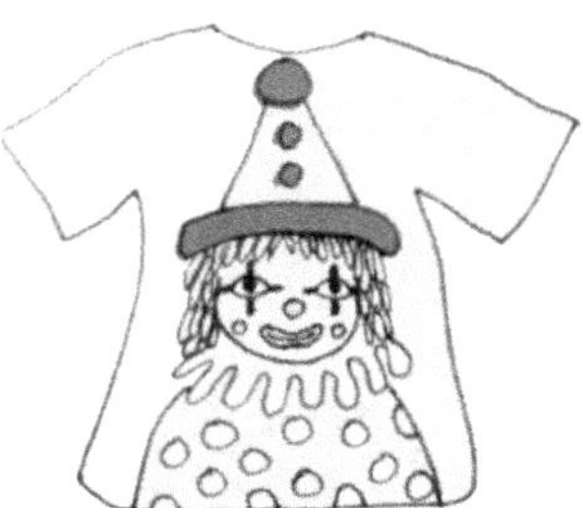

Clown T-shirt

Paint on the clown's face and hat, then sew real pompoms on his hat, sequins on his cheeks and hanks of yarn for hair. Add rows of lace around his neck ruffle.

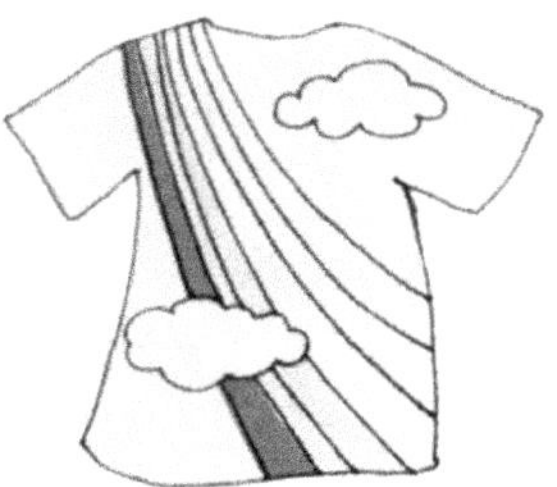

Rainbow T-shirt

Red, orange, yellow, green, blue and purple stripes are drawn on a sky-blue T-shirt. Draw or sew some white clouds.

JEWELLERY BOX

Materials:

Wooden icy-pole/popsicle sticks

Wood glue

Decorations, e.g. gold thread, coloured paper, pictures, paint, buttons, sequins

Step 1: Lay eleven wooden sticks one next to the other horizontally. Then put glue on another eleven sticks and lay them vertically on top. You should now have a neat square — the base of your jewellery box.

Step 2: The four walls of the jewellery box are built up with icy-pole sticks laid flat, not on their edges. This creates an open, basket-like effect. First glue one stick on the left edge and one on the right edge of your base.

Step 3: Put glue on the ends of two more sticks. Fix these on the top and bottom edges of the base. The ends will fasten onto the first two sticks you glued down.

Step 4: Glue two more sticks left and right, and two more top and bottom, and repeat the process until the four walls have built up to a height of about 7 cm (2 ¾ inches).

Once you have finished the box you can make a lid. Do exactly what you did to make the base using eleven wooden sticks.

You may put on a few extra ones for decoration on the top but this is optional.

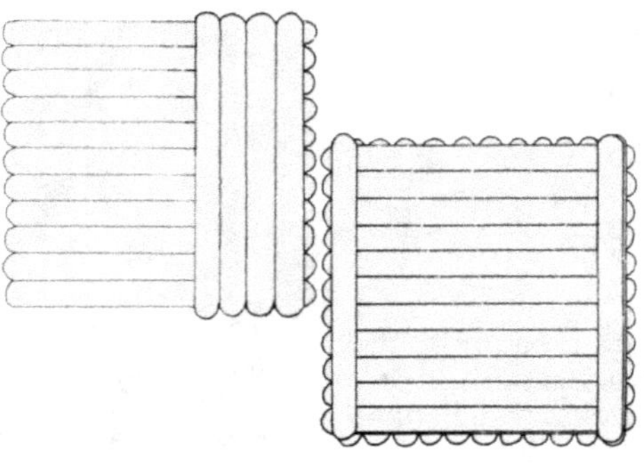

Step 5: Decorating the Lid

This is great fun. On the top you can stick coloured paper shapes or pictures cut from cards, magazines or wrapping paper, and coat them with varnish. You can also put glitter on the top of the box. Painting it is also very effective — you can paint each stick a different way. A nice idea for a lid is if you glue three wooden sticks in the centre and put pictures or someone's name down the middle with paper. Then paint the base of the lid different colours.

Buttons and sequins stuck on also look great and you can even paste gold thread around the edge of the lid.

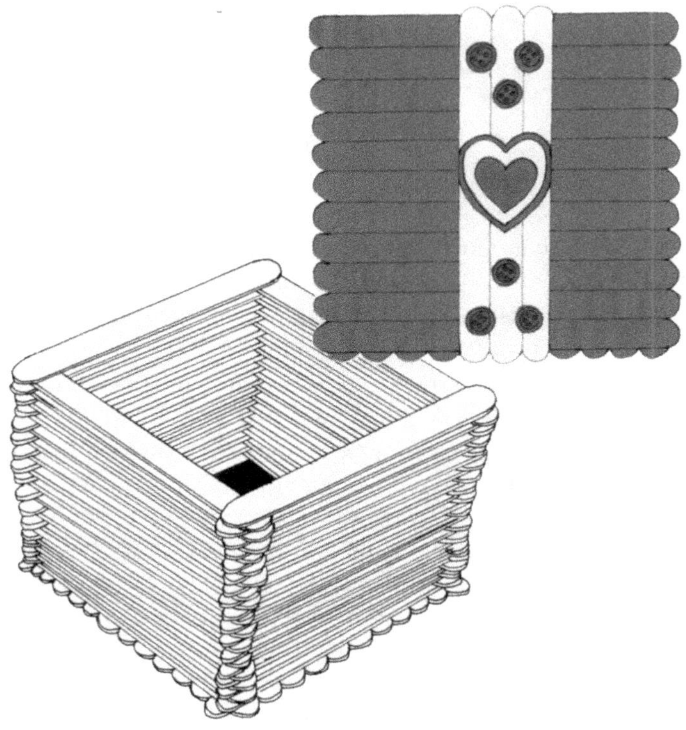

GODS' EYES MOBILE

Materials:

Wooden icy-pole/popsicle sticks
Strong glue
Scissors
Coloured yarns
Two sticks or pieces of thin dowel about 30 cm long

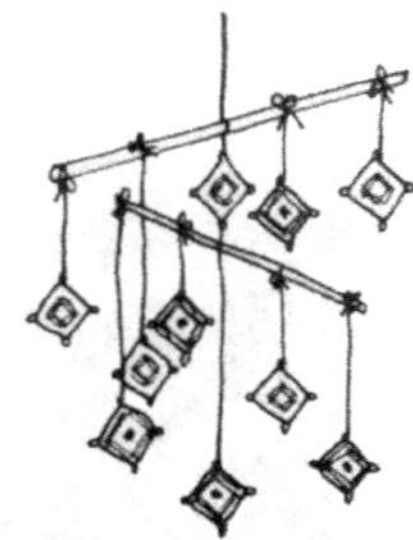

Step 1: Take two wooden sticks and glue them together in the shape of a cross.

Step 2: Tie the yarn close to the centre, carry it around one stick and then bring it up and over it, as shown.

Step 3: The yarn is then carried under the adjacent stick and around it to make a loop on the top side.

Step 4: After you've wrapped about a centimetre (½ inch), turn the sticks over and begin again in a different-coloured yarn, to create an interesting in-and-out effect. Keep doing this until the sticks are completely covered, then tie off the yarn and leave a length of it to fasten it to the sticks.

Step 5: Wind yarn around the sticks or paint them. Suspend one stick from a strong piece of yarn tied in its centre, and suspend the second stick from the centre of the first, so that both sticks are horizontal. This can be a bit tricky, you could ask an adult to help!

Step 6: Make 8 or 10 Gods' Eyes on yarn of different lengths and hang them from the sticks, making sure that they balance each other so that the sticks remain horizontal. If this is too hard, hang them from a coat hanger.

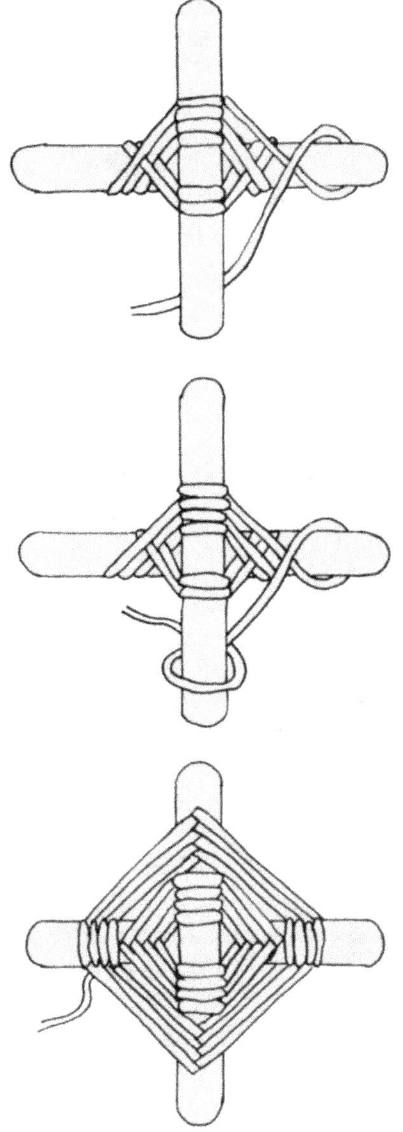

BATIK PICTURES

This project involves the use of hot wax, so ask an adult to help you.

Materials:

Cotton cloth, e.g. an old sheet cut into rectangles
A block of paraffin wax (from hobby shops or department stores)
Small paintbrush
Cold fabric dyes in at least three colours, e.g. yellow, red, blue
Lots of newspaper
Large jars for mixing dyes
Chalk or charcoal
Rubber gloves

Step 1: Place the paraffin wax in a saucepan and put the saucepan in a larger pan of hot water to melt the wax. If you have a fondue set you can keep the wax warm in that.

Step 2: Cover your work area with newspapers. Using a piece of chalk or charcoal, lightly draw your design on a piece of cloth. Some design suggestions are shown here — or you can make up your own.

Step 3: Brush melted wax completely around the design in the places you want to stay white. Where the wax goes, the dye will not penetrate. The wax *must* go through to the back of the cloth. If the wax thickens, reheat it to make it thin.

Step 4: Mix yellow dye in cold water using the directions on the packet. Wearing rubber gloves, carefully dip the waxed fabric into the dye. You will have to scrunch up the fabric to do this.

Step 5: Rinse the cloth in clear water. Do not wring it. Hang it up to drip dry in the shade. The parts not waxed will be dyed yellow.

Step 6: Put a second coat of wax on the places you want to stay yellow, then dip the cloth in red dye.

Step 7: Again rinse and let dry completely. The red dye over the yellow dye makes a lovely orange shade.

Step 8: Put a third coat of wax on the places you want to stay orange. Mix some blue dye and re-dip the fabric. Rinse in clear water.

Step 9: Place the wet fabric between newspapers or paper towels, then press with a hot iron until all of the wax is removed. The wax will soak into the paper and leave bright colours on your design.

You can use batik to decorate T-shirts, dresses, tablecloths and cushion covers, or to make wall-hangings.

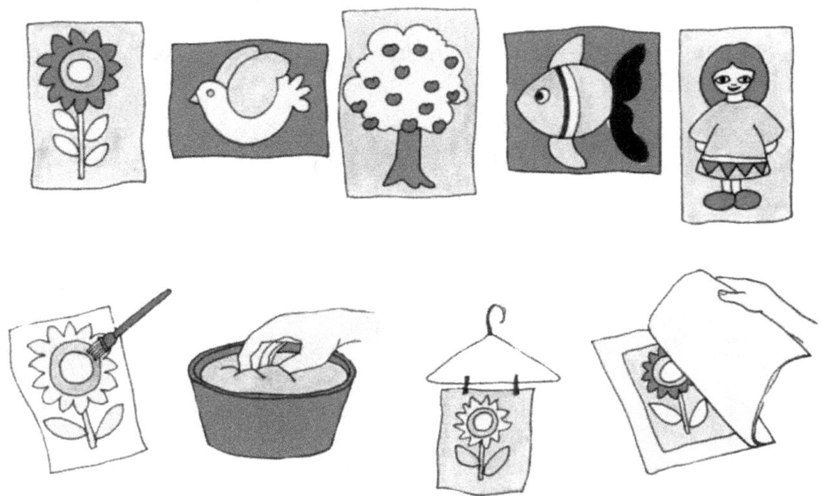

CRÊPE PAPER ROSES

Materials:

Florists' wire
Coloured crêpe paper
Wooden skewer or pencil
Scissors
Thin canes for stems
Green crêpe paper
Strong sticky tape

Step 1: Crêpe paper usually comes in a flattened roll about 12 cm wide. Cut about 14 cm (5 ½ inches) off the end of this roll, and keep it rolled while you cut this petal shape out of it. Leave about 4 cm (1 ½ inches) uncut at the bottom of the shape.

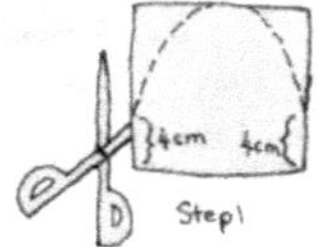

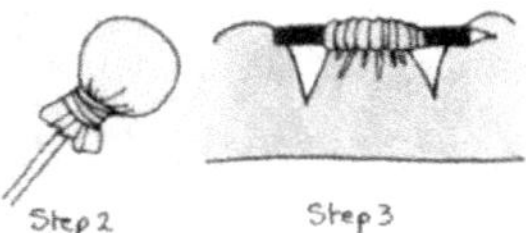

Step 2: Make your flower's centre by screwing up a ball of paper scraps, covering it with a square of coloured paper and fastening it with sticky tape to the tip of the cane. The centre may be a different colour from the petals.

Step 3: Unroll your chain of petals and shape each one. To do this, roll the tip of each petal onto a pencil or skewer and squeeze it tightly together. Slide the pencil out, leaving a bunched roll. Then curve the main part of the petal outwards by stretching the paper with your fingers to make a hollow shape.

Step 4: Stick one end of the chain of petals to the base of the flower's centre, then wrap the chain around and around the stem (staying up near the centre), bunching the petals slightly for fullness, layer after layer.

Step 5: Fasten in place by winding florists' wire around. Cover the wire and the whole stem with a winding strip of green crêpe paper.

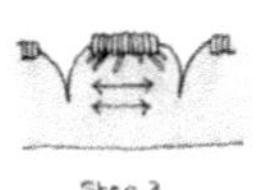

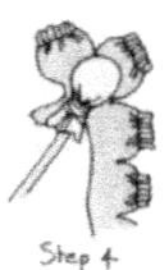

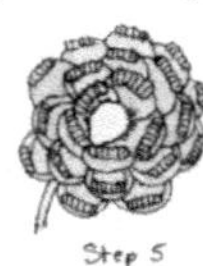

FESTIVE CRAFTS

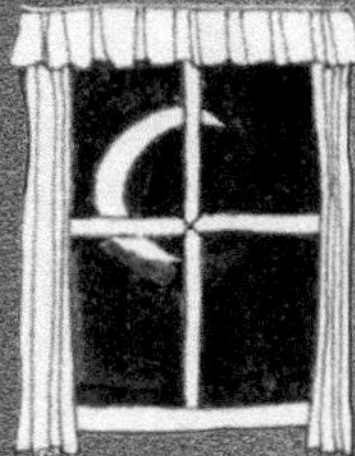

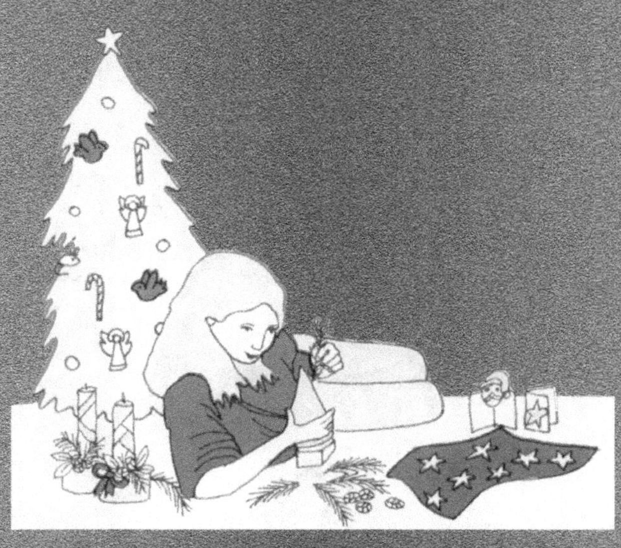

MINIATURE CHRISTMAS TREE

Materials:

A small square block of polystyrene foam such as Styrofoam

A wooden dowel or straight stick

A piece of Oasis cut into a cone shape

(Oasis is a block of porous material which you can buy at florist shops. It supports flowers in arrangements and keeps them moist.)

Tips of evergreen branches such as pine

Miniature ornaments, such as tiny pods and cones painted gold

Plastic food wrap

Step 1: Insert one end of the dowel or stick into the square of Styrofoam. Wet the Oasis cone thoroughly and wrap it tightly with plastic food wrap. (This will keep the Oasis moist a long time.)

Step 2: Push the Oasis cone onto the other end of the dowel, leaving enough of the stick between the Styrofoam and the cone to look like a trunk.

Step 3: Now push the evergreen sprigs into the Oasis cone starting at the bottom and working towards the tip, making sure they are very close together and cover the whole cone. At the tip, stick one branch upright.

Step 4: Decorate the tree with miniature ornaments stuck into the Oasis with wire. Wrap little blocks of different sizes in coloured paper; tie them to look like gifts and pile them around the base of the tree. You can cover the Styrofoam base with foil or coloured paper.

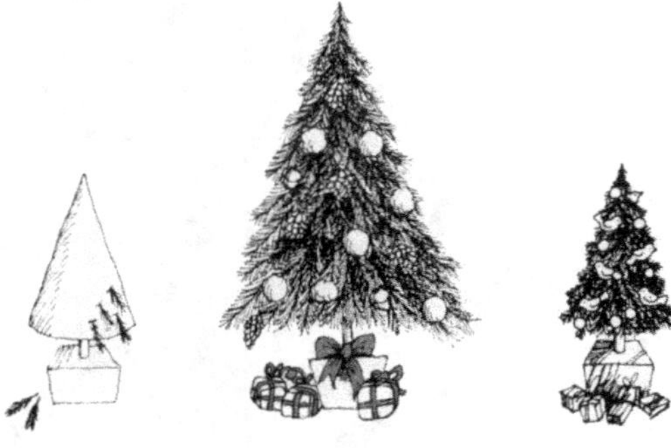

POP-UP GREETING CARDS

Materials:
A piece of thin card about 15 by 30 cm (6 x 12 inches).
Paints or crayons

Step 1: Fold the card in half length-ways and place it on the table so that the folded edge is on the right. Bring the top right corner down until it meets the left-hand edge and use the edge of a ruler to make a definite crease.

Step 2: Open out the card and fold it in half the other way The creased section of the card should be facing you.

Step 3: Fold the card from left to right and pull the V-crease down into the centre of the fold. Next cut off about 4 cm from the top of the card (along the dotted line).

Step 4: Open out the card and the centre portion will pop up. Draw an appropriate design on this pop-up portion and cut around the top where it extends over the top of the card. Decorate your card with paints or crayons, write your greetings and the card is complete.

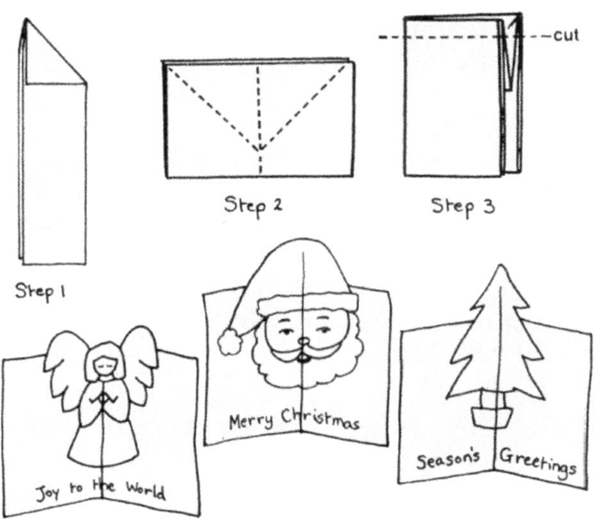

PRINTED GIFT PAPER AND CARDS

Materials:

Large sheets of paper, e.g. 'butcher's paper', coloured tissue paper, or discarded computer paper
Thin white cardboard cut into rectangles
Scissors
Large potatoes
A small vegetable knife
Poster paints or acrylic paints
A paintbrush
Paper towel
Gold felt-tip pen

Step 1: Cut a potato in half, being sure to make a straight cut, as the surface must be perfectly level. Decide on a design you wish to print — e.g. a star, a tree, a holly leaf, an angel. Draw the design on a piece of paper and cut it out.

Step 2: Blot the cut surface of the potato with a piece of paper towel to remove any surface moisture and place the paper design in the middle. Trace around the design with a straight pin, or the tip of the vegetable knife (ask an adult to help), and then remove the paper.

Step 3: With the knife, carefully cut a little ditch about a centimetre deep around the edge of the design, digging out the pulp a little at a time. Next, cut in from the edge of the potato to the ditch, removing the potato in between, so that the design stands up in relief. Blot the surface once again.

Step 4: Brush paint thickly on the raised design, and then turn the potato over and press it firmly on the paper or the folded card. Lift it straight up to avoid smearing the edges. If the edges of the print are smeared, the paint may be too thin.

Step 5: Cover your paper with prints in various colours and allow to dry. Write greetings in your cards with gold pen, and perhaps you can add a little glitter for decoration.

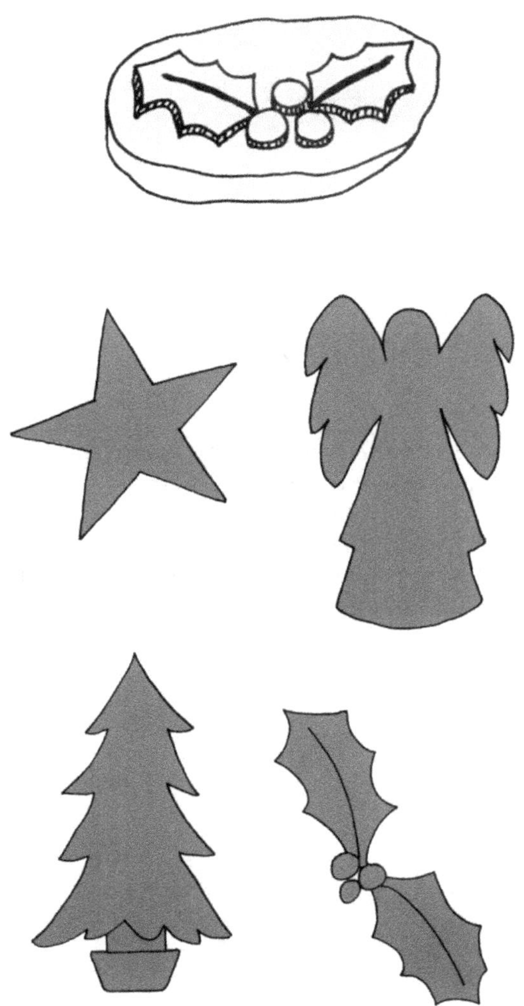

FESTIVE CANDLES

You can either make your own patterned candles to put into the candle holder, or use bought red or white candles. If you make patterned candles, ask an adult to help you because hot wax can be dangerous if spilled.

PATTERNED CANDLES

Materials:

A tall, slim, straight-sided jar, or tin, or cardboard roll for a mould
Coloured wax or coloured candle-ends or wax crayons
A small saucepan
A plastic ice-cube tray
A length of candle-wick or thick string
Cooking oil

Step 1: Melt some coloured wax in the saucepan over a very low heat and pour it into the ice-cube tray. When the wax is cold and set, unmould the cubes by warming the tray slightly in hot water.

Step 2: Coat the inside of the jar or tin mould with cooking oil. Place some of the cubes into it, against the sides. Put the string wick down the middle. Melt a different colour of wax and pour it in (make sure it's not too hot), tilting the jar so that the wax sets on an angle.

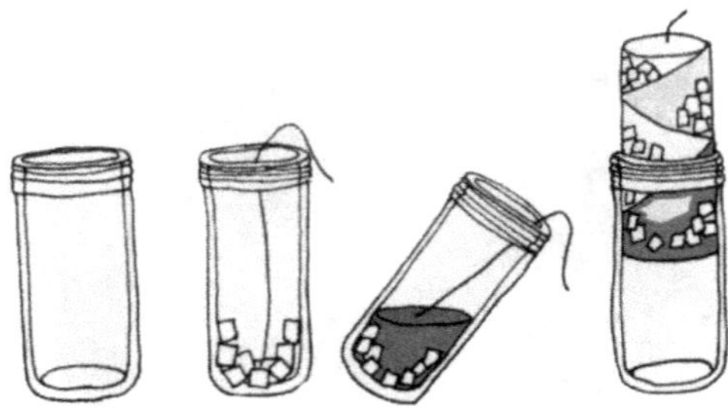

Step 3: After the wax is cold, put in some more cubes, melt another colour of wax and repeat the process until the container is full. For variety, you can also set pretty leaves into the sides of your candle; the wax will preserve them.

Step 4: When the candle has set, unmould it by warming the jar or tin slightly in hot water and sliding the candle out, or by peeling away the cardboard roll. Trim the wick.

CHRISTMAS CANDLE HOLDER

Materials:

A patterned candle or bought candles
Paint or gift wrapping
Plasticine
Green leaves, e.g. pine
A low, wide empty can, e.g. a salmon or tuna can
Red ribbon
Chicken wire
Small gumnuts and pine cones painted gold or silver

Step 1: Paint the can, or else glue gift wrapping tightly around it. Fasten the candle in the middle with plasticine.

Step 2: Fill the space between the candle and the edges of the can with crumpled chicken wire.

Step 3: Arrange the leaves around the candle by sticking them in the chicken wire. Make them no higher than half the height of the candle. Add the gilded gumnuts and cones, and the red ribbon tied in a bow.

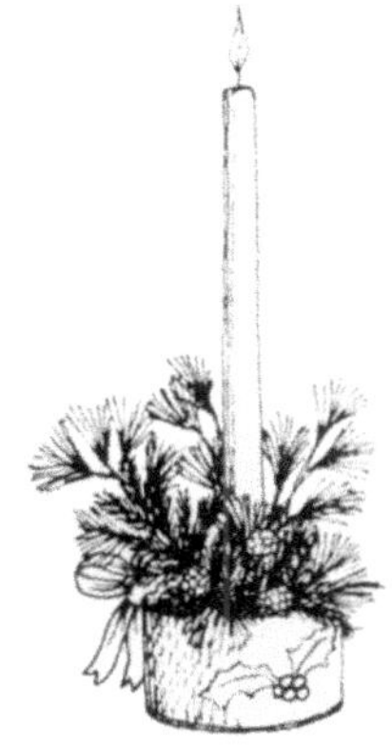

CHRISTMAS TREE ORNAMENTS

You can make lots of attractive ornaments for your tree by painting gumnuts, seed pods and pine cones gold and silver.

Birds, angels, Santa Clauses, stars, baubles, mice, candy canes etc. can be fashioned out of Bread Dough, Polymer Clay or Papier Mache pulp, as shown in this book. Paint them in bright colours and varnish them.

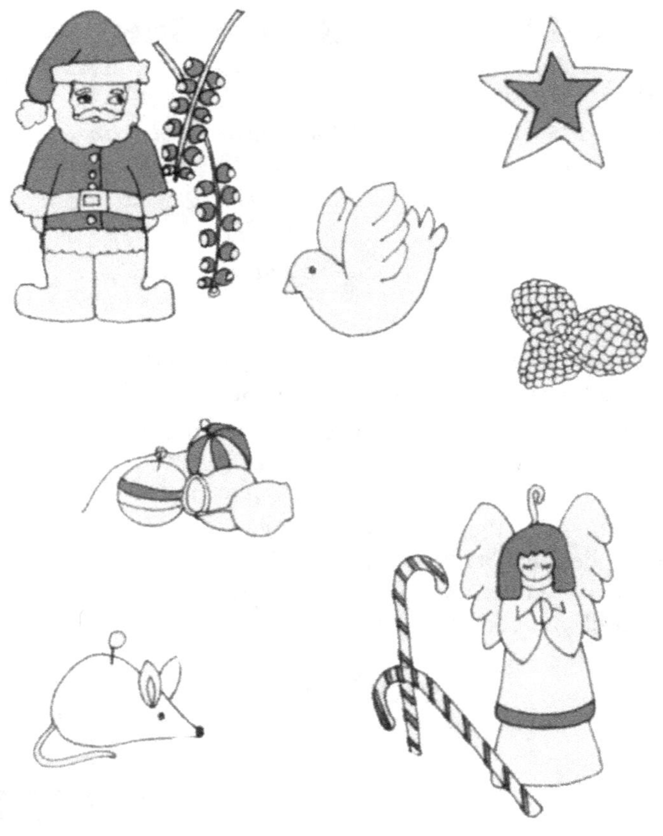

INDEX

SOME MORE BOOKS IN OUR CHILDRENS' SERIES:

The Parents' Time Off Series:

- Kids' Magical Activities
- Kids' Gardening Activities
- Kids' Cooking Activities
- Kids' Hands-On Craft Activities
- Kids' Fun Craft Activities
- Kids' Creative Craft Activities
- Kids' Games Book 1
- Kids' Games Book 2
- Kids' Nature Activities
- Kids' Holiday Activities

Classic Fairytales from Tolkien's Bookshelf:

- Grimms' Fairytales - Illustrated
- The Red Fairy Book - Illustrated
- The Princess and the Goblin - Illustrated.
- The Story of King Arthur and his Knights - Illustrated

Find out more on our website!

www.leavesofgoldpress.com

THE PARENTS' TIME OFF SERIES

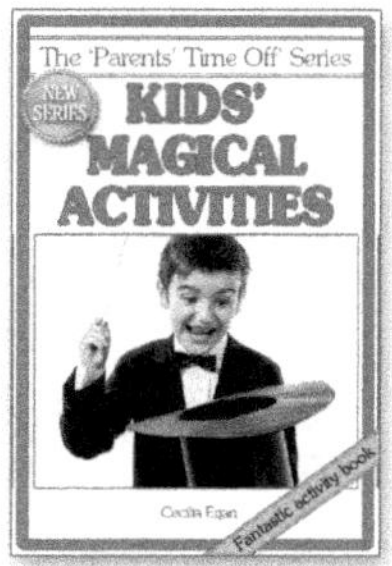

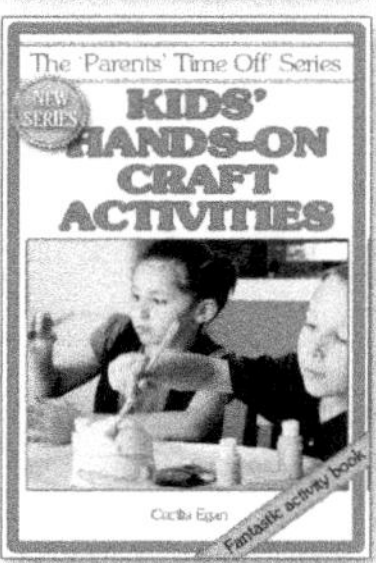

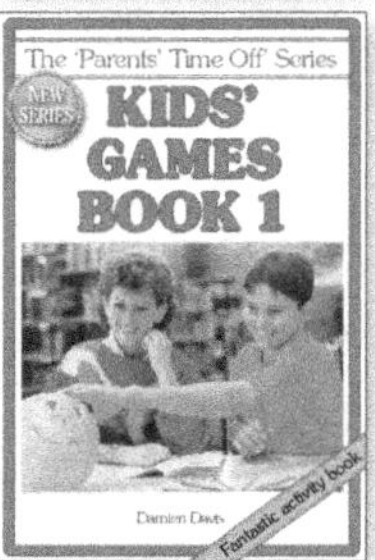

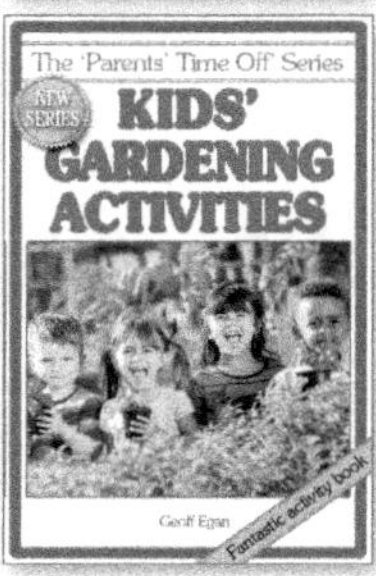

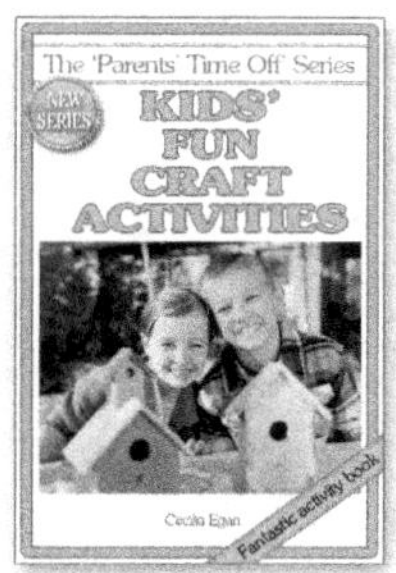

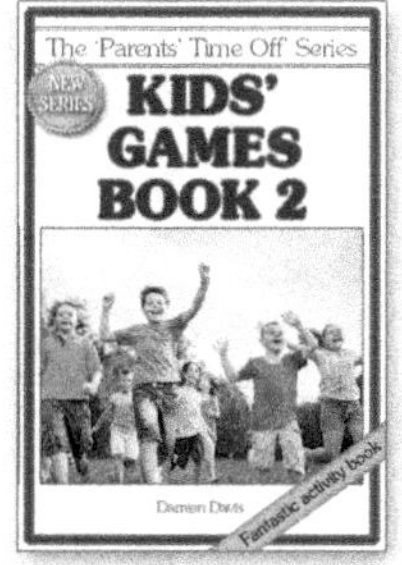

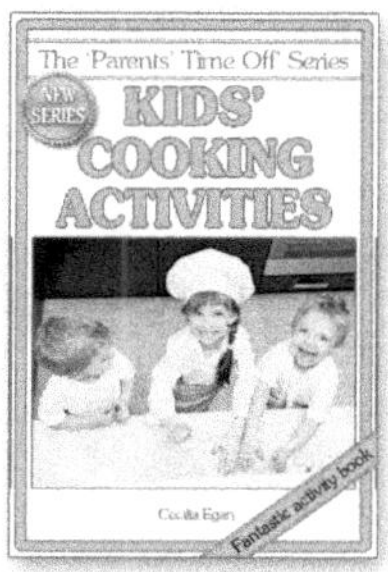

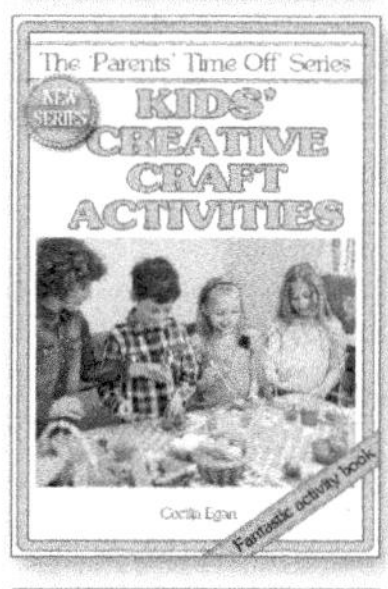

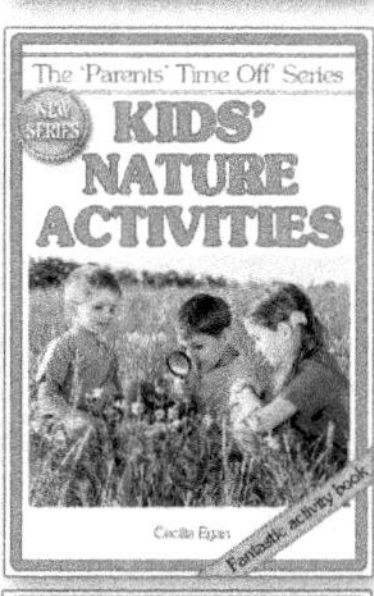

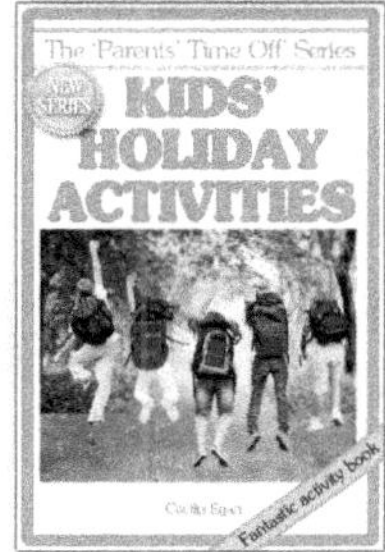

Princess Pam Fell Into the Jam

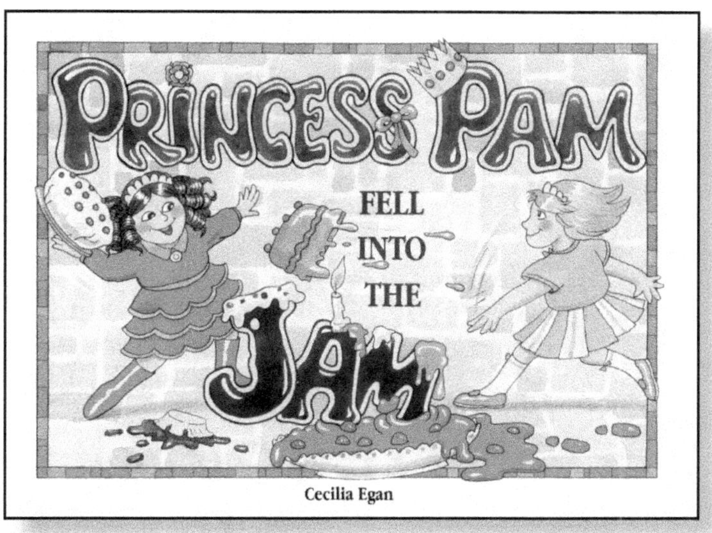

More than a hilarious rhyme, this is a slapstick comedy that causes a riot of laughter when read aloud. Princess Pam and her messy sisters appeal to every child.

The rollicking rhymes, the unconventional story and the lively, detailed pictures combine to make one of the funniest and most original children's books published.

www.ingramcontent.com/pod-product-compliance
Lightning Source LLC
LaVergne TN
LVHW010107110826
845155LV00028B/520

* 9 7 8 1 9 2 5 1 1 0 7 2 2 *